Overwrite Technology

Teach work

By H.A DAWOOD

Contents

nformation and Communication Technologies (ICT) stimulate changes that they involve the whole of social life on a planetary scale. However, beyond the promising speeches that question men and women of the globe as "con-Iconsumers and users of a technological world", the integration of ICT in different countries, geographical regions and social groups does not occur uniformly. The insertion processes are complex, often dual and do not reach all the population by same. Is necessary recognize, by a side, what the expansion from themass media and digital technologies enhance the production, circulation, storage dining and reception of various messages at great distance and scale. But, on the other, to the motorize inequalities on the access to the information and to the knowledge, increaseexisting economic, social and cultural differences. The so-called "digital divide" isdynamic and involves aspects related to inequity in access to infrastructure, supports or connectivity, in the possibilities of interaction and in the potentialities of appropriation significant on the part of users.

By the moment, then, the dissemination from the TIC I know gives on the frame from a "glob-asymmetricalization" [1] promoter of imbalances that exceed the variables merelytechnological. TO weigh from it, the media from communication and the technologies digital from the information have a impact on the configuration the around material and symbolic
From who transit the new century? The TIC intervene so much on the production from goodsand services what on the processes from socialization. His importance lies on the can formediate the formation of opinions, values, social expectations, and ways of feeling, thinkingand Act on the world. A) Yes, on a society where the groups social I know find every time plus fragmented, the technologies from the information and the communication They are channels fromcirculation from representations and ideas on turnstile to the which the population segmented can find points from Contact and Connection. From is perspective, the TIC have a function cultural central: build up the knowledge what the subjects have on the society what hub- so. But I know treats

from a building selective traversed by the saturation from information, by a side, and by other, by the presence from the media massive from communication with concentratetin on the production from contents and a strong imprint from the logic the market.

In this sociocultural context, education tends to behave as a variable what define the entry or the exclusion from the subjects to the different communities. Is what the ambit school follow being a space privileged for the knowledge and interventionon the complex phenomena necessary for coexistence and social change. Is for this reason, the entry of ICTs into the school is linked to literacy in the new languages; contact with new knowledge and the response to certain demands of theworld of work. But the pedagogical integration of ICT also requires training capacities for understanding and participating in this mediated reality. In this sense, systematic training is an opportunity for young people and adults of become both thoughtful consumers and creative cultural producers. Is an opportunity to develop knowledge and skills that mere contact with technologies and their products does not necessarily generate.

The political relevance of the inclusive role of the school around the problem of TIC was made explicit recently on the frame the debate from the New Law from EducationNational. The document submitted for the discussion public posed the responsibilityof the Argentine National State to "guarantee equity in access, since this will depend on the future abilities of the students, in order to make the most of intelligent use of ICT, whether for access to cultural goods or for the acquisitionskills training for the world of work. The school –the text affirmed– "must assume a fundamental role because it is the space where all boys and girls, young and adults can effectively access digital literacy. That's how it went and The school's mission continues to be the entry of children into the literate culture, today it must incorporate the learning and use of new digital languages". In the currently, through articles 7 and 8, the National Education Law (No. 26,206) legislates on is reality. The Condition "guarantees the access from all them citizens/as to information and knowledge as central instruments of participation in a process of development with economic growth and social justice", and maintains that "education shall provide the necessary opportunities to develop and strengthen thetraining integral from the people to it length from all the lifetime and promote on every educate-have the ability to define their life project, based on the values of freedom, peace,solidarity, equality, I respect to diversity, Justice, responsibility and well common".

This scenario invites the school to reflect on the proposals for insertion articular, didactic strategies and institutional ICT management models. But, fundamentally, it challenges her to rethink the forms of transmission of knowledge that are put into play in their classrooms. For the pedagogical integration of ICT to be con- pour into an opportunity for inclusion must be significant for those who participate inher. A insertion effective no I know can give to the margin from the processes historical, culture-rails, politicians and cheap by the which the subjects transit. Needs to reply to

Their realities, worries, interests, knowledge and expectations. Demands give the word tothe students, return them visible and recognize them what subjects cultural on a here and now.

From there the beginning the school Argentina I know worried by "build up equality", by jointo the different on turnstile to a draft common. But the system educational traditional was designed based on a principle of homogeneous supply. Today, although they worry toons remain the same, the new cultural mechanisms of society and theknowledge economy tend to respect particularities. Schools go approaching information and communication technologies in very diverse, negotiating come in the progress media tic and technological, the cultures organize- nationalities, the needs of teachers, generational gaps, and appropriations autonomy of young people and the expectations of the community. Hence, public policies Public laws require taking into account the institutions and the subjects in a situation. When on the present I know talks from equality on the school, I know think on a equality complex.An equality that enables and values the differences that each one contributes as a human being.No. From East mode, the school on so much agency Social I know reinsert on the dynamic cultural.It is revitalized as a fertile public space for the "citizenization of the problems of the communication" [2]. Is what with the integration from the TIC to Projects transverse and S.I.G-nificative, the school is coupled to different movements of civil society that playa role vital on the protection and promotion from the diversity from the expressions from the culture and access to knowledge.

Training on TIC

The incorporation of ICT in the pedagogical work of school institutions is end-stretched out by the Ministry from Education, Science and Technology (Emceed) what partof inclusive policies aimed at reducing the educational gaps that currently exist on Argentina. The inequality from opportunities what suffer youths schooled belonging to sectors underprivileged from the society is conceived what a trouble not only economic but political, pedagogical and cultural. The differences in the possibilitiesnighties of access to technology currently also imply great distances in the possibilities of access to cultural products, information and knowledge, that impact on the construction of subjectivity, future life projects and the citizen participation of the new generations. That is why the integration of ICT in school is not understood from the present proposal as a problem merely technical and instrumental. boarded from a perspective educational and cultural,the incorporation of information and communication technologies in teaching requires the development of analytical, cognitive, creative and communicative skills students, teachers and directors, which allow both the significant appropriation of the circulating cultural, technological and informational offer such as the production of messages required for personal, professional and citizen performance in a pluralistic society. Clever and democratic.

On line with a perspective educational and cultural, then, the integration from TIC to the pro-put pedagogical can be considered what part from a politics inclusive when: considers

to every school What center from extension from the offer technological and cultural; I know worries by the growth from skills no only techniques otherwise as well cognitive, creative and communicate- ties necessary for the performance Present and future from the youths; conceives to the technologyand the processes of circulation and consumption of information or cultural products such as an object of constant problematization; incorporate technology and information into teaching on different fields disciplinary; favors the building from subjectivitiesintegrating the global technological and cultural offer to life contexts; facilitates the exPressure and visibility from youths from sectors underprivileged to through from the productionand put on circulation from posts own what strengthen the identity local; articulates theschool work of integration of ICT and disciplines with practices that involve to the community; and, finally, when it proposes a continuous institutional work that promotes the appropriation of ICT as part of present and future daily life (entertainment, education, communication, work, participation).

On East sense, the proposal what I know presents on East material understands what the trainingof students in ICT requires the strengthening of teaching teams, directors, tives, supervisors and technicians. A strengthening that allows an approach to the new languages and "new cultures", rethink teaching strategies and designnew didactic proposals. It is necessary to reposition the teacher as a mediator of educational processes. Young people need to be guided to achieve productions critically and creatively. But in this task the teacher cannot work in an isolated otherwise conforming equipment under a framing institutional. Without embargo, manysometimes it is the institution itself that needs support, both in training and updating tin of its professionals as in management.

We know that schools in our country are different. Their institutional histories, cultures organizational, experiences from job, styles from management, and contexts from dimes- peon, professional teaching trajectories or interests of the students they host are diverse. A proposal for the pedagogical integration of ICT cannot ignore this diversity Yes aims to be significant and satisfactory. From is perspective, then,pedagogically integrating ICT in the school does not imply focusing exclusively on the use of equipment and tools but in the learning processes, planningand change on the practices and the institutions. The TIC no have potential transformeron Yes themselves. The adequacy to the contexts, the possibility from answer to needs andthe sense what achieve acquire on turnstile to Projects individual and collective they are some from the keys to effective integration.

East material has been developed on the frame the *Component rom training and managementof projects in critical use of ICT in PROMSE schools,* through which the emceed it is proposed to form, train and coordinate provincial technical teams, referentsinstitutional, supervisors, managers teachers and auxiliaries what favor the integrate-tigon pedagogical from the resources audiovisual and computer scientists to spread out on the schools tights belonging to is line from financing.

Inside from their objectives pedagogicalcos main I know find: toast a framing conceptual for the understanding from thecomplexity and features from the culture media and his relationship with the subjects; pose strategies from character innovative to leave from the incorporation from the technologies from the in-training and communication in daily practices; define and have a framework conceptual what East the look and the selection the use and the intervention pedagogical from the TIC on the classroom and on the institution, What contents discipline and What tool from with- Dyed cross, accepting as well diversity from production and appropriations from these resources; favor instances from elaboration from proposals what tend to the promotion of one culture collaborative, with incorporation from the TIC; use and promote the job from

different resources multimedia for accompany and set up new channels from communitycation and production in the development of proposals that account for the construction from knowledge linked to the practices schoolchildren; to incorporate the technology to the classrooms What didactic resource, accompanied by reflective appropriation processes that allow res- ponder to the new demands.

In this work proposal, the formation of teams of ICT referents in the schools play a role central. These equipment they will be integrated by couples technician-pedal- gics that will act as facilitators of work in the classroom with the technologies of information and communication, and which will go through each institution. Their roles will be linked to the training from the teachers, the advice and assistance on design, theimplementation and evaluation of ICT projects in institutions and the coordinationmanagement nation between schools and other institutions. It is to these referring teams of ICT to whom this material is addressed. The purpose is to provide a common framework conceptual and reflection for work with teachers.

In this sense, we know that the challenges for each work group are different because your starting points, possibilities and expectations are. A proposal of existing classroom that intends to expand, an institutional goal that wishes to reformulate Starting out or a new project that you are looking to start are fertile spaces for development of the proposals presented in this material. The pedagogical integration of technologies of information and communication is, as was said, an opportunity to access the knowledge, citizen training and cultural expression. But it is also a opportunity to reflect on daily life, desires and feelings about the world that are built from the public school in our country.

On the route from are pages I know pose Some strokes for to think the changes and the lu- gar from the technology, keys for to integrate the TIC on the school and opportunities what provide some tools digital for buildup and propitiate environments from learning mean- tie. Visually, presents a structure tubular or by blocks. To the side the body central the text appear a column with comments (c), bibliography extension recommended (b), links to pages Web (w) and questions for guide the reflection (r).

This material is only the starting point for a rich and dynamic work, which with the participation of teachers and students, will take on a life of its own in the classrooms.

Introduction

"A new form of society is emerging before our eyes. And this so- society no is something alien to us. Is here, on our lives personal, on our emotions, on the anxieties what we face everyone the days".
Anthony Giddens

There are few stuff on the can insure what exists a agreement widespread. The transformation the world current, the certainty the change and the sensation from uncertainty with respect to the future they are some from they. The sociologist Sigmund Baumann points out what the speed- dad from the transformations, the questions to the truths structuring on the what us vesupported, the processes of de-traditionalization and constant innovation, the great modifications captions on the institutions modern traditional (job, family, couple, gender, Church, democracy, State, civil society, political parties, etc.) and the cult of individuality aremaking stagger the certainties what held the reasons from our *lifetime daily* [3], undermine-do his stability and impacting on the way from to live and from to think the future.

[3] This concept has been widely treated in the contemporary sociology: "When talking from daily life us referee-
We come to that *supreme reality,* to the life of the whole man, to the obvious and normal fabric of the understanding of the world and of

It should be noted that these changes have been taking place since the last century, especially from the second half. As historian Eric Hobsbawm (1999: 18) on his book *History the Century XX,* "that period was the from higher transcendence historyAC from the century, because on the I know record a Series from changes deep and irreversiblefor human life on the entire planet. Beginning with the end of World War II World, let's remember the consolidation and the crumbling the *world bipolar* (com- nest *versus* capitalism); the cycles from increase economic and depression; "the deathof the peasantry" [4] ; the consequent urbanization and revolution in public transport; the rise of professions that required secondary, tertiary and university studies rivers; the growth and rise of higher education, the new female consciousness and the inclusion from the women on the college and on the market the work [5] ; the variation-nes on the settings relatives; the boom from a culture specifically youth; thedevelopment of the mass consumer market, fashion, the recording industry, tele- vision, the technologies electronics, etc. Is say, the role the Condition, the market and from thedifferent institutions social was Changing, and from his hand, the guidelines from organization,the hierarchy from values, the Models from reference, the wishes and the expectations so much from the individuals as well as the communities in their set. [6]

Still finding lines of continuity for the characteristics of the current world in a longer historical time, we could speak of a new type of modernity. For Bauman (2002), the current era can be defined as a "liquid modernity", in which that power and money flow, move, drain, and need a free world from fetters, barriers, borders fortified and controls. On opposition to her, it what the Authorcalled "solid modernity", now disappeared, was built on the illusion that the change would bring about a permanent, stable and definitive solution to the problems. The change was understood as the passage from an imperfect to a perfect state, and the process of modernization was carried out once and not to change more. Liquid modernity have other conception: the change and the innovation I know perform permanently. Baumann exemplifies the difference between both configurations by comparing two characters represented tentative each of these moments sociohistorical and cultural:

"It is understandable that Rockefeller wanted his factories, railroads, railroads and oil wells were large and robust, to possess them fora lot, a lot weather (for all the eternity, Yes we measure the weather accordingtheduration from the lifetime human or from the family). Without embargo, Bill gates I know-ra without pain from possessions what Yesterday it were proud: today it what gives Profits is
The rampant speed from circulation, recycling, aging, discard andreplacement -no the durability neither the durable reliability the product-".

Both cases illustrate in personal stories the macrosocial processes and their respective tive worldviews. But it is necessary to understand – as Hobsbawm (1999: 13)– what the reflection on East world complex have as well for everyone and every one fromusas adults an unavoidable autobiographical dimension:

"We speak as men and women of a specific time and place, who have participated in its history in various ways. And we talk, too also, as *actors who have intervened in their dramas -however insignificantwhat is been our paper –*, what observers from our epoch and whatindividuals whose opinions about the century have been formed by those whowe consider crucial events of the same. We are part of this

What we mean is that, being contemporaries of social events, political, cultural, economic and educational that we try to understand, will speak on our interpretations, the history personal and the brands what the situations us they have left as experience. In the ways of reflecting and knowing the world, it will be pre-feel our subjectivity, what plus what a *source from error* is condition from possibilityof knowledge. The always claimed objectivity is impossible. And the point of view inescapable. Hence, it is necessary to have a certain vigilance about it. Think the world, to rethink the place of the school in the new global socioeconomic context andlocal it implies dialogue with others senses on the world. New senses what they will enteron game in many interactions with young people in the school and out her.

Recognize our positioning no It constitutes a relativism ethical individualistic. Is import-much understand what the relationship subject-object I know gives on the contexts from practice and on the dimension active the knowledge. No I know treats, without embargo, from socialize the sense common. Well East "isa deceptive mechanism that obfuscates knowledge; installs the subject in a supposed objectivelife and you prevents warn clues from change or from anomaly on the interpretation from it real". IsWhat "Yes from the signs the around, alone retain those what agree with ourknowledge, confirm our convictions, justify our (in)actions and coincidewith our imaginary" [7] . By it, for overcome the *obstacle epistemological* [8] what the sensecommon supposed, we will try promote from East material a reading intentional and review,integrate intelligence and intuition, reasons and suspicions to build the path of knowledge through problematization. As well as thinking and advancing in understandings precise, although provisional and perfectible, and suggest a framework to reflect the inte-ration review from the technologies from the information and the communication on the teaching.

We will embark on this path by approaching the contemporary world through a selection of five significant current situations or events. It tra-ta from clues or footprints from something plus big. They are, to the time, five "strokes" what outline alook and make up a frame from situation, a construction site, a *collage* on the I know they can glimpsedifferent plots and textures, densities and dimensions the Present on the we live. Will

Focus at certain moments, we will stop time for an instant, to glimpse in them the movement permanent and the multiplicity from their locations. Let's try, to leave from thesestrokes begin to recognize some from the features the world the we form part.

First stroke: "It important is the chip, Mabuchi"

East is the slogan from a advertising from phones cell phones from 2004. The scene sample toa guy from about five years conversing on the kitchen with his mom. While-after she walks from one side to the other, the boy speaks quickly and firmly trying to convince her: "The chip is it important (from you telephone cell phone). The chip I know remains with allthe information…". TO measure what his speech passes, the camera starts to betray to thesmall, until finally it shows the image of the cell phone submerged in a fish tank. The chip was in the boy's hand, he had been saved from the mischief. "Do you know how say to the future? The chip, Mabuchi", concludes the protagonist.

In this line it is possible to recognize some features of the contemporary world: the development roll technological on base to the prosecution digital from the information; the offer growing from products and services from telecommunications [9] ; the differences generational on turnstile to the appropriation of new technologies, and even the feeling that children, youngand adults speak different languages. Generational estrangement between parents and children,teachers and students, grandparents and grandchildren, is usually evident in the use of language, con-markedly differentiated cultural values and perceptions of the world.

It is necessary to emphasize that generational gaps are not exclusive to this time. Actually, it can be said that the great transformations of the 20th century marked important differences generational The people born before from 1925 They had little bitto do with those who came into the world after 1950. Youth like today we know is a *invention* from the postwar period. Is what to leave from the second half the centuryXX the existence of children and young people as subjects of rights was vindicated and, especially, on the case from the youths, What subjects from consumption. Is as well onpost-war period when a powerful cultural industry emerged that defined young people what recipients from his offer. The increase from the industry musical was the plus spectacle-market, although not the only one, and offered for the first time *exclusive* goods for young people, whothey began to have greater autonomy of decision and historical protagonist. Youth wasa lot plus what a group age what I know differentiated from their greater. According Hobsbawm (1999:331), the culture youth I know converted on the matrix from the revolution cultural the century XX, visible on the behaviors and customs -but on everything on the mode from provide the leisure-, whatI pass to configure every time plus the environment what they breathed the men's and women urban.

Then the differences generational already they were notorious, So What the perception from what thesociety I was experiencing a new moment cultural, on the what past and Presentthey were reconfigured from an uncertain future. In the seventies, the anthropologist Margaret Mead said that young actors were the best prepared to assume the irreversibility from the changes operated by the globalization, the growth iconologyco and the internationalization of society:

"Our thought us bind yet to the past, to the world such What existed onthe epoch from our childhood and youth, born and servants before from the revolutionelectronics, the most from us no understands it what is means. The youthsfrom the new generation, on change, I know resemble to the members from the firstgeneration born on a country new. Must learn together with the youths theshape from give the upcoming Steps. But for proceed So, must relocate thefuture. In the opinion of Westerners, the future is before us. on trial from Many towns from Oceania, the future resides behind, no go ahead. For build upa culture on the the past be Useful and no coercive, must locate the futureCome in us, What something what is here clever for what it let's help and let's protectbefore from what born, because from it contrary, be too afternoon". [10]

The author distinguishes schematically three types from culture according the shapes what taking the trans-mission cultural, and what they can serve us for to think the Present. The culture *postfigurative* isthat on what the children they learn from their greater. The Present and the future is it so anchoredin the past. They are the cultures of tradition. The *cofigurative* is one in which both childrenWhat Adults they learn from their pairs. The future is anchored on the Present. They are the cultures fromthe modernity advanced. The *prefigurative* is that culture on the what the Adults they learn fromchildren; for Mead it is an unprecedented historical moment "in which young peopleacquire and assume a new authority through his catchment prefigurative the future un-known". In this regard, the anthropologist Rossana rebuild (2000) comments that the value ofMead's proposal is to be able to locate it in our time, in societies such as the Latin American ones.White hair where they can introduce oneself simultaneously shapes *post* , *co* and *prefiguratives* . Is say, onthe coexist different modes from be related with the future and the past.

These days, and especially as a result of the advancement of ICT, the school is no longer theprivileged channel through which the new generations come into contact with the information or I know insert on the world. The children and youths have knowledge and un-braids what they learned without intervention from the Adults. By his part, the lifetime from the higherpart of today's adults has lived in a social and technological environment totally different. In this environment, the institutions "family" and "school" maintained a uniqueness from speech, the authority I know built vertically and the practices from with-sumo around from the technologies from the communication I know gave on a context from strong adult mediation. Over the decades, then, are the same configurations. power relations between generations what changes: decisions about the differentaspects of life are not taught or obeyed in the same way, knowledge is not acquire neither nest from the same way. On East sense, the sociologist Emily TentFanfan (2000) states that changes in the balance of power between children and young people and adults constitute one of the factors that put in crisis the old dis-positive what organized the lifetime from the institutions schoolchildren. Eleven Is what the school I hadlegitimate and exclusive voice both to define what was the valuable knowledge for the society as who were the ones who, possessing them, could transmit them.

It is clear, then, that when we ask about the relations between members of different generations we no longer refer only to the interactions of people of different various ages. The idea of *generation* cannot be thought of as an exclusive category.vely biological, it must also be considered cultural:

"It what distance to a grandson from his Grandpa no They are 70 years chronological otherwise seven decades from transformations cultural, social, policies and economiccase It what distance generationally to a student from his teacher no They arethe birthdays that have been celebrated, but the different worldviews of the world they have built throughout their experience. the brands generations are not lodged or outcrop, then, in hair with or without white hair otherwise on the ways from conceive the past, from transit the Present, from imagine the future, to wish, to dream, to relate to others and tointroduce yourself to others. In short, in the processes of constitution from the identity own and the collective from belonging what incorporate marksfrom epoch". [12]

all instances that go from milking to our refrigerator there is research and production of knowledge applied to industry. But the existence of this informationtin in a *sachet*, bottle or carton also speaks of a consuming population that finds positive the involvement of science in most areas ofthe lifetime. Even though Who buy this milk maybe no arrive to understand from what I know treats, value the existence of this information, the transparency of communication byof the company.

TO leave from the years fifty, payment force the *revolution scientific-technical* and I know conform-the science-technology-production system, closely linking advances ineach of the fields. Intensive scientific and technological production in laboratories corporate rights is one of the characteristics of the society of our time. As the sociologist Manuel Castells (1995) explains, information has become input and factor principal on the restructuring from the processes productive. I know treats froma new logic from increase and accumulation the capital. According East Author, "the generate-tin, processing and transmission of information become the mainsources productivity and power.

On the production from goods and services, the systems what process information and the car-nuance from certain chores what before I know performed on shape Handbook They are protagonists.In this framework, knowledge becomes a key input for *competitiveness.* Thus, from the productive system the notion of *knowledge* is put into circulation *competitive,* what have certain features associated to the world labor. I know treats froma knowledge generally developed in companies, focused on problems or on Projects and no on disciplines, linked to needs from application and innovation. Into- it profits professionals from different areas; is subject to diversified quality controls (international norms and standards, social relevance, economic efficiency, the acceptanceconsumer information, etc.) and uses informational networks for its production, circulation and exchange. It is thus, then, that a significant part of the tasks is binds with the generation from information and from knowledge, with the reproduction, adapt-station, dissemination and sale of messages, ideas, systems, images and symbols.

On East context, the schools and universities leave from be the unique centers from progress scientific and the only ones who control the distribution of social knowledge. Its capital-cone- foundation competes with the capital-knowledge generated autonomously by the system industrial, financial, business and military, which have developed their own centers research and divulgation.

Thus, a new map of trades and professions promoted by the new shapes from produce, communicate and manage the knowledge, bound so much to the alphabetize-tin for the world of work as well as the need to reconcile with the new models business. All this, then, translates into very precise demands on the system. Educational on everyone their levels. I know requests modify orientations and contents on functionfrom the training for the job, and increase the levels from quality. Some trends of change impact the way in which the educational process is conceived and organized, marking the orientation of the institutional and graduate profiles. Among these ten- dunces, the incorporation of information and communication technologies occupies a central place for some decades, promoting strong debates around its mode and objectives from insertion. The discussions about from the need from to incorporateICT as a separate subject or as a transversal content, the emphasis placed on the more instrumental or more critical aspects in terms of student training, goals lined up with the training for the job or the training citizen, the visions

plus centered on the use from it informatics or those what do higher emphasis on it mule- time media They are answers to the relationship school-knowledge, according the different demands,that have a strong impact on teaching proposals. There is currently aa certain consensus on the need for the school to train in ICT thinking of the skills development and promotion of continuous learning with inclusions what contribute to the integration of modalities.

However, beyond the decentralization of the places that produce what is considers applied science, it is important to always remember that the people there work, belonging to different fields of knowledge, have been trained and continue to be command in the educational system.

In this way, in the daily work with ICT in the school, it begins to be necessary saree pass from the notion from "society from the information" based on the technologies frominformation and exchange on a global scale, to a notion of a "society of knowledge" foundation" that, contrary to the globalizing representation induced by the first, as Armand Mattel art (2006) points out, highlights the diversity of modes of appropriation cultural, politicians and cheap from the information and from the knowledge

Intelligences connected

Traditionally, the image public from the science and the technology he was dominated bythe achievements of individual intellectuals. Today, by contrast, some of the jobs scientists plus shocking they are the result from the collaboration from groups. [*] Thefollowing sequence summarizes East change.

• For centuries, the fathers of modern science were related through invited colleges. sibles, is say, formed part from a community from researchers whose exchange of ideas represented the basis of scientific advances. Although the scientists based their works in others and communicated with each other, finally publishing alone. many great- des ideas They were attributed to some few thinkers influential What Galileo, Newton, Darwin and Einstein. Consequently, the traditional way of doing science in modernity dad (until the Second War World) I know describes What a serine from nodes isolated.

• On the second half the century XX, the science I know went back, plus and plus, a job group. AA good example of this is the famous couple of biologists Francis Crick and James Watson, who discovered the structure of DNA. They certainly weren't the only ones. They themselves they made couples with others scientists setting up networks from knowledge. Thejoint publications documented these collaborations giving birth to schoolsinvisible, replacing the connections hidden with co-authors published.

• Currently, although collaborations rarely dominate the way of doing science as numerous as that of the international consortium of the Human Genome Project [**], a large part of the research fields require this type of collaboration. From In fact, the size of teams that do collaborative work is growing, pouring the exercise scientific on a net densely interconnected.

Networking, cooperation and communication are not limited to the activity but are characteristic of social life and the construction of societies. Cities. Beyond this, the interconnection of people and organizations through networks computer science offers a new chance: the from multiply, What it says Derrick from Kerckhove (1999), the "intelligences connected" on function from objectives common.The greatest transformative potential of these technologies lies in the possibility of givingsupport to networks and spaces that allow communication, the creation of spaces for the collaboration and the building from knowledge and the interaction Come in people.

[*] Barabbas, Albert-Laszlo (2005): "Network theory - the emergence of the creative enterprise", *Scientific American,* Vol. 308.
[**] The Human Genome Project (HGP) consists of mapping all the nucleotides (or pairs from bases) and identify the 30,000 to 35,000 genes presents on he. The big amount from information what generated and generates the PGH required the development of electronic databases to be able to store and managejar from shape plus easy and fast all is information. *the GDB man genome Database:* http://www.gdb.org/

By part from every society. Jesus Martin Barber (2002), to the same what Mattel art, spice-list on issues of communication and culture, highlights:

"Our societies They are, to the same weather, societies the unknownuncle, this is the no recognition from the plurality from knowledge and competenciesthat, being shared by the popular majorities or the minorities,you laugh natives or regional, no is it so being incorporated What such neitherto the maps from the society neither even to the systems educational. Butthe subordination of oral and visual knowledge currently suffers a increasing and unforeseen erosion that originates in the new modes of production.duct ion of knowledge and new writings that emerge through the new technicalities, and especially of the computer and the Internet".
Third stroke:Argentines on the Exterior
"Experiences from Argentines on the Exterior and the dilemma from return or no to the country" is the qualification froma Article published on *Clarion* the 7 from

August from 2006, what treats no on a curiositythe moment, otherwise on a theme recurrent from make Some years on the diaries plusimportant the country. On general, the grades count by what I know They were, excuse me they live, which one is his relationship with the country what the receives, on what they work, etc. A variant from East type from grades is, by example, what do the scientists Argentines on others countries. Is common, as well, find- bring on the stories what the technologies from the communication, especially Internet -with their possibilities from chat and videoconference–, constitute a resource important for keep daily contact with family and friends. Added to these stories is the creation of websites what The exile from Gardel.org, homeless, immigrants Argentines: the community fromArgentines by the world, etc., what offer a space for to share the experiences on the former-foreigner, So What the memories from the Argentina native. On East sense, the new technologies they contribute substantively to the communication and to the Contact.

From what talks East stroke? Talks from the globalization economic, from the migrations andof the different reasons and forms of movement of the population in the world (for recruitment of professionals in multinational companies, in search of better living conditions, wars, political reasons, etc.). Remember, too, the inequalities between countries –and within them– [13] , as well as the vicissitudes to buildsea a new lifetime on a place different to the from origin, the conflicts social, culturaland of coexistence that this generates. This seems to be a moment, as Martín Bar-baron (2002), "in which men from very diverse cultural traditions *emigrate in the weather,* immigrants what they arrive to a new was from temporalities very diverse, butall sharing the same *legends* and without models for the future. away to installa single or homogeneous culture, the intensification of transnational cultural flowsthem seems to drift In a world of character increasingly mongrelized".

ICTs, thanks to the speed of processing and transmission and their connection to networks around the world, have changed the conceptions of space and time. Is spoken of the *space of flows* that compresses time until it becomes present continuous and it compresses the space until the terrestrial distances disappear. In addition to helping maintain the link between family and friends, the interactive digital network connects placesdistances with their distinctive socio-cultural characteristics and brings together various modes from communication. The permeability every time higher from the borders information-nalos It allows the emergence from new communities from interests and values what sidestepthe geographic variable. This phenomenon expands among young people, where music or the games on net I know transform on cores from communion. The use from the TIC reinforces sentiment-cough from belonging, to through from the pages Web, the mail electronic or the channels from chat; is a way from enlarge ties social and cultural outside the neighborhood, the town or the country.

It is important to bear in mind, as Martín Barber (2002) points out, that the procedures economic and informational globalization are reviving the question of the cultural-ethnic, racial, local, regional identities, until turning them into a protagonist dimension of many of the fiercest international conflicts of the latest years, to the weather what those same identities, plus the from gender and age, is-are reconfiguring the strength and meaning of social ties and the possibilities of coexistence on it national and it local. Martin Barber add what it what the revolution

technology of this end of the century introduces into our societies is not so much a quantity unusual quality of new machines but a new mode of relationship between the processes symbols that constitute the cultural.

Sociologist Dominique Dolton (1999, 2006) emphasizes that understanding between cultures, symbolic and political systems, religions and philosophical traditions it is not achieved simply by speeding up the exchange of messages. Inform, express or transmitting is no longer enough to create a communication. For the author, the "victory of the communication" comes accompanied from a change on his condition. Is less a process, with a beginning and an end – in the manner of a message that goes from a sender to someone who receives it–, that a *challenge of mediation, a space of coexistence, a device that points to amortize the meeting with several logical what coexist on the society open.*

On East context the role what assume the proposals from teaching on turnstile to the TIC result fundamental. By a part, because have the possibility from follow, continue expanding the limits the classroom from the classroom. By other, because on a world what places on Contact to people from different places, learning to communicate with sensitivity towards others (expressing oneself, listen, dialogue, understand, exchange, reach agreements, cooperate, resolve con- conflicts with understanding mutual, I respect and solidarity) is crucial for the training ethics and democracy of the citizens of the 21st century.

Quarter stroke: The planet on danger

"The planet on danger" is the qualification from a Article journalistic what sample a case from
trouble overall : pollution, heating from the Land and change climate.

TO ends from the years seventy, the deterioration from the terms environmental on Some pointsthe planet it gave place to the beginning from a large debate on the roads what the humanity there was taken on pos the growth socioeconomic, and even to the mobilization from the citizensfor these topics. The environmental problem was then thought of as an addressable issueon terms from disciplines, extension the knowledge scientific and instrumentation frommechanisms cheap and financial. By example, I know thought what the pollution I know solved _ through the creation from systems from decontamination designed from the science,the creation from money for to ease the investments necessary and the taking from measures What the fines for place Brake to the Actions polluting. East focus biased and frag-minted failure. Today I know understands what I know treats from a trouble the knowledge, what demand the reconceptualization from the relations Come in society and nature:

"The environmental crisis, understood as a crisis of civilization, could not understand counter a solution by the via from the rationality theoretical and instrumental whatbuild and destroy the world. Apprehend the environmental complexity im-apply a process of reconstruction and reconstruction of the thought". [14]

This is how the environmental problem and others, such as cloning, genetic modification, AC from animals and floors, the instrumentation productive from those progress to big scale,

they have been defined as *scientific problems of a new type* [15] . In this line we can recognize part from his complexity: the "costs the progress", the force the market,coexistence between people, national sovereignty, the role of States, the diplomacy, money, citizen participation in public affairs, movements social, democracy, respect, the future.

By other side, the damage caused by Some products scientists and the use from the sciencefor political, ideological and military purposes contrary to the humanist designs that had always been awarded to him have provoked the concern of the citizens for the ethical relevance of those human activities and their results. The treatment of problems from new type bring with him questions theoretical about from the limits from the science western, his alleged objectivity and his presentation to the margin from the values.In other words, this conception of scientific knowledge as shape legitimate and valid approach to reality.

These problems put on evidence the need from build up a new type from know-I lie, from exercise scientific and from participation citizen on these affairs. I know precise *dialogue between disciplines,* between different cultures and their respective knowledge, between the Sciences and the knowledge laity from the lifetime everyday. The delimitation from the knowledge on the different fields from the Sciences constituted on their first stages a process necessary and Useful for know the reality. The *specialization* ha brought big benefits, without embark-go, started to become, recently, on something what hinders on measure growing the understanding of the problems. According to Edgar Morin (1999), there is an inadequacy every broader, deeper and more serious between our knowledge disunited, divided, shared and the realities and problems that are increasingly multidisciplinary, transversal, multidimensional, transnational, global, planetary. According the Author, I know needs to a "reform the thought" what allow link, contextualize, globalize and, to the same weather, recognize the singular, the individual, the concrete. Likewise, hegemonic scientific knowledge, considered the unique capable from introduce us on the knowledge real, is Changing from place to the be the *man common* the what claims his space on the discussion on the pertain-Inc. the knowledge scientific and their Applications on the lifetime Social.

On East stage the school occupies a role central on the training from citizens, is say, from people able from to think the *complexity* from the situations, from address them to leave from day- logos respectful of differences, of trying valid solutions for the majority, of putting on play the intelligence, the intuition, the creativity, the solidarity and the ethics, and from assume

The responsibility that this implies. *The role of the school is thus fundamental such and irreplaceable on the promotion from shapes from to think, from communicate and from Act what allow young people address the challenges of his time.*

Fifth stroke: *Live 8* , organized by *mark power you history*
TO weigh the increase economic on many regions the world, no I know ha finished
with the trouble from the poverty. we did mention on a stroke previous to what the
world globe-lysed sample what the inequality Come in the countries rich and the poor
is every time higher, SoWhat the gap on the inside from every one from they. *Live
8* was a event to scale world,organized by *Make poverty history* (Make history the
poverty), the two from July from 2005, on thewhat I know they performed concerts
from rock on different cities the world the same day, mobilityhoisting Thousands
from people and synchronizing the transmission on alive and direct to everything the
planet.East stroke us talks from the globalization, other time, and places from
manifest the observation fromNestor Garcia Canclini (1998): "it fragmentary is a
feature structural from the processes globalizers . The globalization is so much a set
from processes from homogenization Whatfrom division the world, what reorder the
differences without delete them".

Is interesting stop us on East event. The 1 from July from 2005, the Kingdom
Unitedassumes the presidency from the Union European and the first Minister Tony
Blair I know commits to place on the schedule from job for the future the following
topics: trade just, reduce-tion or condonation from the debt external from the
countries plus poor the world, increase thehelp economic, commitment for to help
to fight the AIDS. The two from July I know makes the concert *Live 8,* under the
same slogans, in order to install in public opinionis schedule from topics and
achieve the Pressure world on the leaders from the countries plus rich. Bond,
Leader the group U2; Bob geldorf, from Pink floyd, and others stars international-
nals the rock and the show mobilize a cause politics. Blair appear on the channel
from videos musicals met for to converse with a group from youths on these topics.
The rock, the politics, the opinion public, the transmission to everything the world by
radio and television. From the site from Internet, what's more from provide
information on the theme, I know promoted differentActions, What by example use
a bracelet White What symbol from accession to the cause or Send post electronics
to the different leaders politicians. Among the 6 and the 8 from July I know gather
the presidents the G8 (group from the seven countries plus rich the world: state Uni-
two, France, Italy, Germany, Canada, Japan, Kingdom United, plus Russia) on
Gleneagles,Scotland. The 7 from July I know produce the attacks terrorists on the
town from London.

The development of this topic is beyond the limits of this material. we only want highlight three issues. In the first place, the significance of the *synchronicity* of the events. Second, how these situations of international terrorismcontribute to the climate from uncertainty and unsafety what we come describing. By last-mo, let raised the question by the youth on East, their differences and similaritieswith the youths Latin Americans, which we will continue to treat continuation.

Young people are increasingly traversed by global electronic flows, which pro-see a part every time plus important from the materials on what I know they build thenarratives and versions from it Social and his own identity what individuals. [16] The culture

World culture, mass culture, does not act only at the moment when it is faced with the screen, but is expressed in everyday life. When the young hum the songs fashion toons, when they wear a T-shirt with inscriptions, when they buy the clothing *from mark* , already no is it so forehead to the apparatus from radio or television. Is it so looking at each otherface each other, they are communicating beyond the presence of the medium. As the anthropologist Maria Teresa Quiroz (2003: 64) says, it is in the body, in the face,on the way from speak, on it what I know eat, on it what I know sings, where the culture from massesis displayed at every moment. According to Regulon (2000), the costumes, the music, the access to Certain emblematic objects today constitute one of the most important mediations for the identity construction of young people, which is evident not only asvisible marks of certain ascriptions but, fundamentally, as a way -in- three others- from understand the world. They are shapes symbolic, and no by it less real,to identify with equals and differentiate oneself from others, especially from the world adult. This is how the cultural, that is, the realm of meanings, goods and cultural products, today has a leading role in all spheres of life. Is in the field of cultural expressions where young people become visible as social actors. [17] Ecology, peace, human rights, the defense of traditions tions, the expansion of consciousness, rock-even anonymity, individualism, hedonism or consumerism– become flags, emblems that group together, give identity and establish the differences between the same young people.

Is important clear out what the youths no constitute a group homogeneous? No everyone thewhat have the same age participate from the same "class from age", already what no everyone com-depart the same features and experiences vital (to form couple, to work, attain economic autonomy, study, etc.). Beyond these generic particularities, the teenagers and youths They are carriers from a culture Social done from knowledge, values, attitudes, predispositions, which usually do not coincide with the school culture and, in especially, with the program that the institution proposes to develop. As Tenuti says Fanfan (2000), while the school program maintains the traces of the funs- rational (homogeneity, systematicity, continuity, coherence, order and sequence unique, etc.), the new generations They are carriers from cultures diverse, fragmented, open, flexible, mobile, unstable, etc. The school experience often becomesdo on a border where I know find and face diverse universes cultural.

Then, a shape possible from approach is situation is to work with the products and theprocesses from production cultural from the youths, for try *hear* what is it so trying from say to through from their music's, his poetry, their *graffiti;* what is it so trying from tell to the SW-society on terms from settings cognitive, affective and, especially, policies. [18] The cultures juveniles they act what expressions what encode, to through from symbols and idiomsdiverse, the hope and the afraid. The challenges what the youths you pose to the company-dad is it so there, with their strengths and weaknesses, with their contradictions and disarticulations.

Let's go back to the " *Live 8" trace* to see how rock and the youth cultures that were de- developed in the last century, especially in the hands of the media, they respond on East new century to a announcement politics and global done by stars of rock. We also find some indications of a new type of political participation.tic from the youths: I know observe the trend to the accession, with a selection careful,

to specific causes and not so much to traditional militancy. According to Regulon (2000), these "commitments itinerant" must be read What shapes from performance politics no institutetutionalized, as a "politics in lower case". Young people, despite their differences, share the characteristic of having a planetary, globalized consciousness, which can be considered what a vocation internationalist. Nothing from it what happens on the worldit is foreign to them. On the other hand, they prioritize the small spaces of daily life as trenches for boost the transformation global. Regulon it says what such time I know the can accuse them of being individualists, but they should be recognized as having a "general ethical-political principle". roost": the explicit acknowledgment of not being bearers of any absolute truth in Name from which to exercise exclusive power.

Capturing these meanings will allow us to advance in the understanding of the different ways in which the youths participate real or virtually on the space Social and on the lifetime public, and sowork with them, from school, for citizenship for the 21st century.

Crowds smart *(Smart mobs)*

Between 1999 and 2000, Howard Rheingold began to notice that people were using cell phones and the Internet in new ways. In different cities of the world the young news and no so youths used is technology for get organized spontaneously on turnstile to Actions collective, from those from nature politics until the pure fun. People come together, cooperate in ways that were not possible before because they have with devices capable of data processing and communication. Without embargo, are technologies able from enlarge the cooperation already they have proven bebeneficial and destructive, used both to support democratic processes and for terrorist actions. Despite this, for Rheingold there is a great opportunity for *intelligent crowds* : the alphabet, the cities, the press did not eliminate the poverty neither the injustice but they made possible what I know they will create ventures cooper-ratios for to get better the Health and the welfare from the people. Must remember what themost powerful opportunities for progress are not in electronic technologies. Case otherwise on the practices social.

Rheingold, Howard (2002) *Crowds smart,* Barcelona, Geisha. Page personal: http://www.rheingold.com/ (On English)

Some articles on these topics, published on Educate:

Flash mobs and *smart mobs* events: Crespo, Karina (2006) "The Web: a platform for the creativity?"on:http://weblog.educ.ar/espacio_docente/webcreatividad/archives/001559. Pap [Last consultation: 8 from February from 2007]

Use of cell phones and text messages: Manzoni, Pablo (2006) "Cell phones as interfaces cultural",on http://weblog.educ.ar/sociedad-informacion/archives/007547.php [Last consultation: 8 from February from 2007]

As well:

Gruff at, Carolina (2006): "The posts from text, a practice global?" on http://weblog. Educ.ar/sociedad-informacion /archives/007861.php [Last consultation: 8 from February from 2007]

A stroke plus: The "revolution" from the TIC

On East latest stroke, us interested highlight, for the ends from East material, the importance of what I know considers the *revolution* on the technologies from the information and the communication.

"The technological leap that allows information to be digitized and that encourages the hypothesis that in the last thirty years there has been a informational revolution, is sustained at the same time in the project of the vengeance from brackets, logical industrial, cultures organizational, markets and regulations from the main industries related with production, treatment, processing, storage and distribution of information. Convergence is one of the main concepts that deserve to be elucidated because it is a sum of processes that affect the marrow of the informational society. [19]

The analysis of these *convergence processes,* which refer, in general terms, to the trend towards the merger of companies from the world of entertainment, journalistic, production of software and hardware, telecommunications, in large corporations, exceeds the scopes from East job. Without embargo, we want pose two reflections. The The first circumscribes convergence to the merely technological plane. The possibility of sending photos through cell phones or consulting *online editions* , which include videos and audios, from the world's newspapers, or listen to radio broadcasts by Internet, is produced thanks to information digitization processes. The *conversion agency* is, on East sense, the possibility from what a same means, medium be vehicle from texts writings, sounds, images, videos. Today on day can hear the *radio* on a radio, on a computer via the Internet, on a mobile phone or in recorded form on a reader of MP3. It is as if the media could no longer be identified by the devices.

The second I know refers to the question politics from the convergence and from the globalization from the culture what a organizer from the memory and the I forget. The question would -on words by Armand Mattel art (1998) – if the digitization of knowledge could impose a new criterion from universalization, a mode peculiar from to think and from feel, a newshape from organize the memory collective. To the respect, Beatrice carol (2002) raises:

"The acceleration what it affects the duration from the images and from the stuff, affect-ta also memory and recall. Never like now, was the memory such a spectacularly social topic. And it's not just about the memory of crimes committed by dictatorships, where social memory maintains the desire for justice. It is also about the recovery of memories cultures, the construction of lost or imagined identities, the na- ration of versions and readings of the past. The present threatened by the acceleration wear becomes, as it goes on, a matter of the memory. Between the acceleration of time and the memorialist vocation there are coincidences (...) We resort to images of a past that are each more and more images of the latest. To summarize: speed culture daddy and nostalgia, oblivion and anniversaries. That is why fashion, which well captures the era, cultivates with equal enthusiasm the retro style and the pursuit of novelty".
The technologies they are the element evident from the communication and transport, what I know haseen, a cultural model. With ICT there is a different kind of perception of the world, from to live, from to work, from to teach, from learn. What's more, what poses Walton (1999):

"Few sectors so vital to contemporary society are so present what the communication technological. The history the telephone, the cinema, radio, television, computing has only a century of lifetime. But the breakups introduced by are techniques they have been so violent and I knowthey have led to cape so quickly, what It seems what is it so there from forever".

However, technology is not enough to change communication within the society and a lot less others problems What the from the coexistence cultural on the breast of the international community. There is a difference between the speed of circulation from the posts and the slowness from the changes on the practices social. we will resume Easttopic later, however, we want to raise the issue using words arms of the same author:

"If a communication technology plays an essential role, it is because symbolizes or catalyzes a radical rupture that exists simultaneously in the culture of that society.

In principle, what is an undoubted potential for the pedagogical task is the possibility possibility offered by new technologies to democratize production and convert their tools on instruments from Author. The possibility from *personalize* these resources it will depend from the contexts from appropriation significant what every institution school can build up Come in everyone the agents and subjects what participate on their Projects from integration.

The schools and the teachers on a world from changes:
The point from departure for begin to work
On the strokes we have indicated some elements characteristic the world current and, to pair- shot from there, we have raised questions and reflections with the end from can articulate and build up new proposals from teaching.

The education specialist Andy Hargraves points out that teaching, at present,it is a profession that suffers the tension of two forces, among others. On the one hand, it is expected that teachers are able to conduct a learning process that allows the development of capacities for innovation, flexibility, commitment, and, in this sense, to become promoters or promoters of the information society and the knowledge and all the opportunities it promises. On the other hand, it is expected that the teachers and the schools mitigate and counteract problems from our weather, whatthe deep inequalities economic and on the access to goods symbolic, the excessiveconsumerism and the loss of the sense of belonging to the community.

The integration of ICT in education can generate new pressures in development of the usual tasks of a teacher and in their ways of teaching. Work with tech-audiovisual and computer technologies requires acquiring new knowledge, going beyond the own discipline what I know is teaching and keep *updated;* So What to offer, onthe teaching of the subjects, approaches consistent with the changes that the new technologies provoke on terms from production scientific, and relevant on relationshipto global problems. It implies reflecting on one's own practices and designing spaces and times in which the teaching will take place.

"The course of educational progress is more like the flight of a butterfly than the trajectory of a bullet", is the metaphor with which the education specialist PhillipeJackson (1998) describes the activity in the classrooms and refers to unforeseen situations, unique, unstable and indeterminate on the is necessary improvise. As well happens- rá this with the TIC. Here, the expertise, the creativity and the sensitivity -all Aspects from theintuition–, balancing the forces of reason, reflection and explanation, will be avaluable source to retrieve to orient the teacher task. Twenty

We have already begun to raise it: cultural changes run at a different speed than the innovations technological. It same happens with the training teacher and the practicespedagogical It important is undertake the way from the exploration and the experience-tion for the incorporation from the new technologies with the clarity from what are no They arean end in themselves, but means and ways of acquiring more polished, refined forms ofunderstanding. Have on mind East target will allow avoid the pyrotechnics, the sensationalism andthe havoc from it what Gaston Bache lard denominates "interest impure" or the false centersof interest that distract the student from genuine knowledge.

In the context of incorporating new technologies in the classroom, the questions fundamental when thinking about a teaching proposal remain: why what, for what and what to teach?, excuse me organize the teaching?, what and excuse me evaluate?,
From what mode must educate for to get better the condition human? We aim foreverto drink decisions substantiated and consistent and to plan, understanding what this fun-coin, what it says Pierre Bourdieu (1997), What a "frame" and no a "Gallows". Open,flexible, reviewable, the plans must function as work guides, sincethey are, in the words of Dino Salinas Fernandez (1994), "hypotheses that are put to the test",especially when for him teacher the use of ICT is something new.

Let's keep going now toward the following pulled apart, where we will present some keys forto integrate the ICT at school. I.
Keys for to integrate theTIC

First key: Build up the relationship with the technologies
The perceptions and expectations that we have regarding the virtues and potentialities characteristics of new technologies influence the type of approach and use that let's do from they. According research recent [21], the teachers agree on recognizeas positive aspects that ICTs facilitate the pedagogical task, improve

the quality education and expand opportunities for access to knowledge. On the other hand, Many perceive what aspects negatives, the sensation from "dehumanization from the teach- mania" and the belief from what the technologies they can encourage the "familyism" on the students.

Faced with this field of opinion, it is opportune to remember that technologies have some parameters for individual and social action. That is, they facilitate different types from Actions, interactions, organizations, learnings, etc., and hinderothers. This is, in a few words, the definition of *affordances* [22], a concept that does not has a literal translation into Spanish but we could say that it is understood in termsrelational min: technology offers us certain *opportunities* and we create, we share meanings, renderings, values, and we develop activities and applications
Favorites around from they. On East sense, on the use, on the relationship what we establishwith technologies, they change us and we change them.

Is important highlight, as well, what the context on what the interaction with the technology of- rare intervenes significantly on the definition from the experience? Our link with thetechnologyno I know makes from shape isolated: the diverse patterns from adoption and from use resultfrom the different practices social on the I know insert, and no from the technologies on Yes miss-more. The representations cultural they play a paper outstanding on the perception Social from theposition and the nature from the technology, the exercise to perform with her and the values what I know give to the meeting. This is a idea important what Many authors emphasize for no incurring on the *determinism technological,* according the which the technology is the only cause from the changes cognitive, from the practices social, from the ideas and from the shapes from to live on society. On is line from thought, many they fell on the simplified Explanation from what the writing, theliteracy and the printing press - especially - brought about religious freedom in the West,the revolution industrial and scientific, the origins from the democracy and the capitalism, etc. On opposed, others authors they have shown what no is the technology from the writing on Yes mis-ma the what cause developments cognitive new, What by example: categorization, memory, reasoning logical, etc., otherwise the processes from schooling involved, the assessmentSocial from are activities and the conformation from devices institutional what the push and stimulate. 23 East is one from the senses on what we pose what the relationship with the newtechnologies I know build. Is by that, as well, what on East module we go to speak from theTIC on terms from *opportunities* , from possibilities from action perceived on turnstile to they, from challenges, and no so much from effects What something what we can predict.

Create contexts from learning with TIC
In order to achieve greater expository clarity and, at the same time, trying to avoid what according to what has been said would be a reductionist view of the matter, we will order and pro- In this section, we will problematize some of the contributions or opportunities of the new technologies according to different approaches.

From a perspective instrumental, we could say what the main contributionsfrom new technologies to human activities are concretized in a series of functions tons what facilitate the realization from the chores, because are, be the what be, forever require certain information to be carried out, a certain process- I lie this and often, of the communication with other people.

On terms general, the new technologies facilitate the access to the information on mu-guys and assorted topics, on different shapes (texts, images fixed and on movement, sounds), tothrough from Internet, the CD ROM, the DVD, etc. AND as well they are instruments what allow:

process data quickly and reliably: perform calculations, write and copy text, create bases from data, modify images; for it there are programs specialized: leaves spreadsheets, word processors, database managers, graphics editors, images, sounds, videos, multimedia presentations and web pages, etc;

Automate tasks;

Store large amounts of information;

Set up communications immediate, synchronous and asynchronous 24,

To work and learn collaboratively;

Produce contents and publish them on the Web;

Participate in virtual communities.

Now well, plus there from everything it what we can do, which would the opportunities in the educational field? One could begin by stating that what allows us to move forward in a new understanding is to see that ICTs are a set of tools with which the individual interacts from shape active forming -What propose Gabriel Silo-mon, David Perkins, and Tamar Globe son (1992), technology researchers and education – an *intellectual association* that enables you to perform tasks more efficient and in less time, and also use them as "tools" to think" [25].

In the last two decades, the perspective of "distributed cognition" has gained strength. Gives". That is, to consider human intelligence as distributed beyond the realm the organism own self, encompassing to others people, leaning on on the media symbolic and taking advantage of the environment and artifacts. In Perkins's words, it would be the "person na-more" the environment. That is, the person can improve their *performance,* expand their capabilities or go further, achieve in-depth changes in their understanding processes. Zion. TO the TIC what offer a *association* or *collaboration intellectual* I know the ha called "instruments cognitive" or "technologies from the mind" because potentially allow the student to think at a level that transcends the limitations of their cognitive system. For the authors mentioned, "the construction site from a person on collaboration with the technology could be much more 'intelligent' than the work of the person alone". [26] They warn, without However, that collaboration requires effort and that if a superior development is sought, above, the student must participate in a committed way, with voluntary attention (in "non-automatic" way) and direct the task met cognitively. Solomon (1992) points out what is *association intellectual* is analogous to the situation what I know arouses when a group of people brings together their mental abilities to jointly solve a problem, pose a strategy or create a design complex. According the Author, "Some they will dominate certain topics and by externalizing it they will give the other members of the group from use processes what no could use alone". Now well, dice East type from association, can ask us where resides the intelligence. The Author Explain: "I know could argue that intelligence is not a quality of the mind alone, but which is a product of the relationship between mental structures and internal tools. Telectuals provided by culture. Perkins (2001) comments that thinking and learning distributed in the person-more appear more clearly in situations in which an authentic and wide inquiry is developed: a student who elaborates a test, a advertising what think a Bell, a director what makes a film, a engineer what designs a bridge. According East Author, on education, usually, the focus

And center on the person "soloist", what uses encyclopedias, books, texts, materials forstudy, but to execute he is seldom provided with anything other than a pencil and paper. Already what for the Author the person soloist no is plausible on the lifetime real, emphasizes whatthe schools they should to help to the students to handle *the art from the cognition distributed.* In addition, the effective use of the environment does not happen automatically, only because it is there, available. If not taught, students tend to ignoresome from the top applications from the "structures from support physical, symbolic or Social" whatis it so to his scope. By example, the abstracts, Titles, indices and the knowledge from the textual structures are part of the symbolic support system to carry out a reading effective. Without embargo, without training on strategies from reading, the students nothey can take advantage from they and usually read linearly from the beginning until the end.

If we think about ICT, we find opportunities to cultivate all kinds of skills related to the ingenious distribution of thought and learning. The *keys* they are, in some way, an orientation in that sense.

Many times it has been suggested that, given the growing increase in available information,noble on Internet, already no would so important to teach contents otherwise skills forhandling that information. However, from the perspective that we are presenting However, this distinction is unfounded, since a fundamental aspect in the art of distributed cognition is the teaching of knowledge. Let's stop at this point. In general, the understanding of a discipline does not only entail knowledge the "level the contents" (acts, procedures), otherwise as well it what might calledknowledge from "order higher", about from the strategies from resolution from problems, styles from justification, Explanation and features investigative the domain on cues-thion, because is East level the what affects on the ability from do, from sort out problems,to propose approaches, etc. These strategies and models provide the main paths from which to choose the relevant behavior in the domain, and they are the that infuse meaning to the activities related to it. Lacking the structure oforder higher, the performer se go limited in their options. Agree with Perkins,

"A person-centered-plus perspective points out that the parameters and basic trajectories of human development can change depending on what could commonly be considered nuances of the environment and of the relationship of the person with him. And surely it is possible to imagine an educational process captive what I know East on higher degree toward the person-plus, strengtheningstudents to accumulate more knowledge and art in relation to the cognitive resources provided by the physical and human means that surround them; actually empowering students to buildaround him his personal "more", his own environment for a program that

On synthesis, the sense from build up the relationship he by the side from to teach to to take advantage of thesystems from support on situations authentic and give the tools for the knowledgefrom higher order.

Now, broadening the look with a social and political perspective, the schools that sign to the youths to do a use significant from the TIC and to take advantage of the systems of support to cognition, will open the doors to new possibilities of access to a higher flow from information, greater occasions for the close up to sources from teach- acne and opportunities labor. Because what we will see on East module, the technologies from the information and the communication no They are simply a means, medium or a tool

for develop the intelligence, otherwise a space multidimensional, public, collaborative, for the building from ideas, concepts and interpretations, the organization and the action. The TIC they contribute a space what can integrate and complement the chores the classroom, special- mind in the experimentation and learning of other ways of knowing and other ways to express themselves, to communicate and to make themselves visible. Also, the greater availability of information will be better utilized if young people are taught to ask questions and trim the problems with novel, pertinent and significant approaches (knowledge-higher order mind). Last but not least, we are facing us potential occasions to enable, encourage and prepare young people for the participation in social and public life with their own ideas and criteria. Thus, the eldest and better access to the opportunities what provide the ICT would contribute to the democratization

Media for the participation
Howard Rheingold -Author already mentioned on East material- think what the

new ten- neology, What the phones cell phones and the computers on net, they can be used What means for participation in democracy. Here we will summarize some from their proposals with relationship to East theme.

Learning to use these technologies, communicate and organize can be the most important load-bearing competence citizen what the youths must to incorporate. Public voice is a way of uniting media competencies and commitment civic. Young people who participate in online social networks access other spaces of the public, since they not only consume but also create in digital environments: they search, adopt, I know appropriate, invent shapes from take part on the production cultural.

• Young people often guide each other in the use of ICT, but they also need guidancetoing about how to apply these skills in democratic processes. The mediafor the participation they can be a tool powerful for encourage to the youths toengage, with their own voice on issues that concern them. Take them from the expressionZion private to the public can help them to turn into the self-expression on others shapes fromparticipation. The public voice is learned, and it is a matter of conscious commitment to a public active, plus what a simple diffusion from posts to a audience passive.

• The voice from the individuals reunited and on dialogue with the voices from others is the base sheath-mind of public opinion. When it has the power and freedom to influence public decisions and grows from open, rational, critical debate among peers, can be a instrument essential for the governance.

• The acts from communication they are fundamental on the lifetime politics and civic from a from-democracy. Showing to the students excuse me use the TIC for report to the public, givesupport for causes, organizing actions around certain issues, the means for participation citation they can insert them on their first experiences positive from citizenship.

• The production on the media is different from the production from, by example, goods economy- monkeys, because have the ability from persuade, inspire, educate, guide the thought and beliefs. The technical power of communication networks is important because it multipliesthe capabilities human and social preexisting from to form associations what make possibleActions collective.The networks electronics allow learn, argue, deliberate, get organized to scales a lot greater and to rhythms to the before no was possible. The culture participatoryit should focus on expression and involvement in the community. These newcompetencies what I know associate to the sphere Social from collaboration and participation must nod- tares on the literacy traditional, the skills techniques and from thought critical.

Of society at large and would provide students and communities with a vat-lord added to their own education, training and development.

The teaching and the technologies
Can say what, on shape parallel to the diffusion from the media from communication and the new technologies in the world of work and leisure, educational systems they have tried, with higher or less success, include them on the practices from teaching. On li-nears general, I know ha match from a vision centered on the possibilities the means, medium, for to motivate to the students and facilitate the understanding of the content curricular.

Notwithstanding the foregoing, it is observed that the incorporation of new technologies in the education generates, with certain frequency, "cycles of failure". [27] When a technology is developed and thrown to the market, arise various interests and factors what tend to apply it to the solution from problems educational. From is shape, I know generate expectations what no I know they comply. It grows the perception from what the use is inadequate and unproductive vow, producing the paradoxical effect of reinforcing the old educational molds that were intended transform. This I know would explain, Come in others factors, by the belief from what the incorporation of new technologies *per se guarantees* educational change and justifies. Is it what I know denominates *focus techno centric.* OR, by the contrary, the trend to *assimilate* new technologies into existing educational practices and use them to do that what matches with the philosophy and practices pedagogical prevailing

The inclusion from new technologies would achieve result a innovation Yes were accompanied from changes conceptual on the conception from his use and from the reflection on by what and for what use them, which They are the contributions and what type from learning I know can promote with they.

It is important to stop for a moment at this point to emphasize the need to take into account the *human dimension* when seeking to promote transformations of this nature. In the adoption of ICT, not only are considerations about learning opportunities, but also *people issues* involved at process and institutional frameworks in which it is produced.

The ways of thinking and the ways of doing, of carrying out the work, are associated, among other things, to the technologies used (books, chalk and blackboard, etc.), and are deeply rooted in people –teachers, administrators and students– and in the institutional cultures. This is part of what is called *tacit knowledge, practical knowledge, implicit theories* or *practical schemes of action* . Anyone from are denominations, making emphasis on Some aspects plus what on others, pointsto explain what I know treats from a knowledge what alone can be formalized partially,that has been accumulated over time through learning processes of the own practice pedagogical, and what I know apply in view of a variety from situations concrete andunrepeatable, articulating complex answers.

[28] They are personal implicit theories aboutteaching and learning that have also been reconstructed on knowledge pedagogical elaborate and transmitted on the training. Are theories or schemes unspokenhave determining force in relation to practices, in the sense that they allow regulate them and control them, and they also have a certain stability.

In short, this is a type of experiential knowledge, represented in images or schemes, from character subjective, personal and situational and to the time own self from a collectiveprofessional. Keeping this in mind allows us to understand that teaching is not simply Apply a resume and comply with the objectives from contents, because permanently We develop tasks that cannot be ruled by procedure manuals orby planning's. To consider the knowledge tacit I know returns fundamental when I knowpromote change processes.

This way of understanding what shapes and sustains the principles of action do-in turn, allows us to understand that the incorporation of a new technology may entail profound transformations in entrenched ways of doing things and the revision from Some assumptions on the knowledge and the disciplines, on the to teach, the learn-right and how we learn to teach.

Likewise, we must consider that by incorporating ICT and changing the proposal of teaching also modifies, on the one hand, the type of learning and performance that we wait from the youths, this is, his *condition from student.* AND, by other, I know the embarkin other uses of technology to which, perhaps, they are not accustomed (or, directly mind, no they have Dyed access). The investigator on education Gary Fenstermacher (1989:155) says that "the *central task of teaching is to allow the student to carry out the chores the learning"* [29] – to the denominates "student"– and give support to the action fromstudy. Is say, the Professor should instruct to the youths about from the proceduresand demands of their role as a student, who, in addition to performing the learning tasks, "It includes treat with teachers, get by with the own companions, front facing forehead tothe fathers the situation from be student and as well control the aspects no academicsof school life."

We understand that they, through activities they have carried out, evaluations what them they have been presented, the styles from the teachers to the what they have Dyed what adapt-and the routines of the institution, have also developed a *tacit knowledge,* some ways of *being a student* and, of course, a series of strategies and "tricks" toplay the play from the relationship pedagogical Then, to the be modified the chores from I learned-zone, the routines, etc., they will have what join to the change and advance toward new modesfrom "study" and toward the incorporation from the TIC What support physical to the cognitionand ways of learning to exercise citizenship. That is, even if they have contactout of school with new technologies, they will have to learn to learn with them, use them in other contexts and for other purposes, and meet the challenge of thinking outside the box.Modes new.

This is another of the senses in which we say that the relationship with technology must be build it.

The youths and the new technologies

Another aspect that we want to raise for this construction is derived from the above recently and from the observation on the approach and use of ICTs made by the youths what have access to they. On first place, the youths they learn to use themin everyday life, by trial and error, from the game, informally, implicitly, intuitive, visual, wondering and providing Come in Yes instructions simple,

Tricks and recommendations, with specific purposes of information, entertainment and communication. Unlike many adults, they quickly understand the *language of buttons* and navigate with ease in the complexity of computer networks. It seems that, as Jesus Martín Barber and German Rey (1999) say, they are gifted of a "neuronal plasticity" and a "cultural elasticity".

Secondly, it can be affirmed that they are practices that tend to become widespread among them for being a symbol of belonging to certain groups. [30] That is, beyond easethey find in managing these technologies, there is a kind of encouragement to use them for be a source of social differentiation.

Lastly, recent research indicate that young people, within their framework of possibilities, they use a wide spectrum from media and appliances. These I know distinguish come in"foreground media" and "background media". The former are the focus of attention, while what the seconds make up a environment nice on the what to work and fun-throw up In addition, they frequently use two or more at the same time. This capacity isdenominates *multitask.*
The learning on turnstile to the possibilities from the technologies
One last perspective, in which we will propose to reflect on the construction from the relationship with the TIC, points to think about them on the frame from the culture and the society. IsIn other words, technologies are developed in contexts other than school and we relate to them in other areas as well.

A process repeatedly verified in media history indicates that, whenthat story begins, people establish a bond with the new medium that is solve predominantly on the Contact, bound to the fascination what produces approx.-mares to the novelty technological. On a second stage, they start to articulate a consumption discriminated by content and thematic areas. It is only in a third moment when the medium is in a position to assume variations in the expression of the contents andgive way to differentiation in the ways of counting, in the aesthetics used, etc. to me- did what I know go developing those stages, appear the differentiations on the appealto the recipient and in the segmentation of recipient profiles.

East is the sense on the what the relationship I know build: let's think, by example, on the his to-estuary the movies and the television. The experimentation and the learning on turnstile to their codes andpossibilities expressive, by part from producers and filmmakers. AND to the time, the answerof the public and its gradual *learning to see* and become familiar with them. The first movies butts I know they seemed to the theater, the first programs from television they were what the radio, etc. On is line from reasoning is logical to think what the applications initials from the TIC turn onaround better-known pedagogical forms.

Evidently, thinking about the new is possible from the heritage of the past and question the paradigm existing. Is a chance for generate propositions for the renewal the order settled down. But with the ideas new or renewed as well reform-poplars our reality Present and future, because no only we know plus, otherwise because I know have opened doors for others territories no acquaintances. This is a challenge, a bet and a chance, because can drink the tension what I know shape Come in the certainty and the uncertainty dumber what a authentic fuel for to think, do science or create. [32]

The lesson we can learn from the filmmakers, producers, directors in the media and ICT is that they get involved with technology, experiment, they search, they study, they see what others are doing about it, they try to innovate, in a and return with the audiences, publics and users. The expressive forms in the cinema and the television, so what everyone the developments with TIC no arise from a time and for forever: I know go renewing, building. We think, so, what the incorporation from technologiesof information and communication to teaching can be perceived as a opportunity for significant change and not as a response to social pressure to technology update.

In short, understanding the social, cultural and historical dimension of the changes that happen on the shapes from record and transmission from the knowledge built sociallytea us It allows understand by what the technologies from the information and the communicationare not understood as *one more tool* but as a profound social change and structural on the shapes from conceptualize and conceive the world what us surrounds; and by itso much, on the shapes from to access, learn and know the around. Having on bill islook, we will have elements new for rethink our assumptions pedagogical and

Decisions about what, what for, why and how, that guide the inclusion of ICT in theteaching. Reflecting on this social and cultural framework also provides us with the chance to define a use with meaning and what add value to the proposals.

Second key: The volume from the information

Internet is a net world from computers interconnected what share informationand resources. In everyday use, the terms *Internet* and *World Wide Web* (from the English, "spider web from width world"), known as well What the Web or the Net, with capital letters, I know employ indistinctly. Without embargo, with the end from can to take advantage of the potential educational what are technologies offer, must to know what no They are it same. The Net is a system from information a lot plus recent what employs Internet what means, medium from transmission.

Whether or not we know how the Internet works, one of the ideas circulating is that it is like a great library, where we can find almost anything. There is a perception unlimited availability of information, voices, points of view, resources, etc., which can be overwhelming. So much so that this phenomenon is referred to in thespecialized texts such as *hyper information* , *overabundance of information* , *data smog* , *avalanche* , *flood,* etc. [33] It should be noted that there is a substantive difference Come in *information* and *knowledge* : is lies on the exercise cognitive from the subjects. Isa lot the information to the what can to access, but other thing is the knowledge cons-trued on base to her, well East involves processes idiosyncratic for his appropriation andtransfer, and I know elaborate on base to a net from connections significant for a subject,in a specific situation and in a specific context of practice. [3. 4]

What we mention on the key previous, basing on the review to the schematic transmit-Zion from knowledge understood alone What information (data, definitions, etc.) what the students they should acquire (memorize), Many authors and teachers put the emphasis onthe growth from skills complex, What develop on the students the spirit critical and skills for the driving from the information, already what for to stock information is it sothe machines, what it do better. Without embargo, East enthusiasm by divide the chores Come inbeings humans and machines us can do to forget what we need memorize, remember,for to assemble a base from information and knowledge from order higher what us will allowlater, Come in others stuff, configure our criteria for evaluate the data what let's find on Internet. The thought no I know gives on the empty, otherwise what is driven and supported by the knowledge acquired, so much on the shape from acts specific what on the beginning fromorganization and reasoning. What it says Emily Tent Fanfan (2005: 115-116):

Arguably, this emphasis on the development of complex faculties, when he from the hand from a depreciation from the idea from education whatappropriation (and

no what memorization) from knowledge and capital cultural,on general, can have consequences negative. On effect, the preference former-collusive by the creativity and the capabilities critics can stay on goodintentions when I know autonomies and I know opposes to the idea from education what
appropriation from the fruits from the culture and from the civilization [...] The creativity and the conscience review constitute concepts empty Yes no go accompanied bya strong emphasis on the domain from those tools from thought and fromaction what the men's they have developed, encrypted and accumulated to it length from his history. On any change from the exercise human, so much scientific-technical as well as aesthetic or sporting, are more likely to invent andcreate the what I know they have appropriate from those elements cultural previously developed [...] The to know accumulated have this virtue: no alone is knowledgedone, otherwise as well method, strategy, instrument, resource for to criticize and overcome it dice. This is a characteristic from the culture contemporary. Onothers words, when I know treats from knowledge and competencies complex, the reproduce-diction is intimately bound to his own production renewed. The culture complex I know preserves and transform on a same movement".

What we are suggesting is that the teaching of these skills should be carried out together with the knowledge of the first order and those of higher order.

Skills for the driving from the information
A) Yes what we need understand from some mode excuse me the librarians order and tasting- Logan the books (and everyone the materials what can find on the libraries) forgive with that what can serve us, for find information on Internet must learn-right to use the tools from search and understand his logic. A from are tools,the plus used, they are the *engines from search*. Basically, we entered the words key and what result is probable what let's get hundreds from Thousands from references, even though noall the is it so on Internet. Us we find her forehead to two problems. By a side, the sites invisible to the engines from search (Watch the box *Internet unseen)* and, byanother, the problem of relevance. The information appears disordered and fragmented.No exist rules structuring. The search engines allow find the information, but no the organize. This can carry to the bewilderment. By that, many times, the abundance from information no I know translate necessarily on a increase the knowledge.

The objective is, then, to distinguish what is useful, what is credible, what is interesting, what is important, evenwhat to times I know have the sensation from waste a lot weather on check triviaor information little bit would be. Nicholas bubbles and Thomas Callister (2201: 62-72) they speakfrom *hyper reading* What the ability from "find and from read on shape selective, evaluate and question what is found, that is, to make their own connections between the wounds, place on doubt the links what others provide, wonder by the silencesor the absences". Therefore, the authors emphasize:

"The ability review for read the information on shape selective, evaluate itand questioning it is one of the fundamental educational challenges that ran the new technologies".

Specifically, what skills does seeking and finding the information needed involve? Ta? Edith Lit win (2004), a specialist in educational technology, suggests:

Identify the nature of the information.

To elaborate the terms for perform the searches (and for extend them: a from thefeatures of the Internet is that a thing leads to another).

Implement strategies from search (return to search engines, pages from links, etc.).

Set up criteria for to select the material on function from the purposes and thetask conditions.

Evaluate on what size this type from information is useful to the purposes of the homework.

Validate the material selected on relationship with the context from production and on relay-tin with the knowledge and the methods of the disciplines involved.

Carry out validations every time plus adjusted (selection gross and fine).

Decide to continue with the search or not.

These actions that involve searching and finding can be done by the teacher to see- lecture the material didactic for their students. East will be able be offered from modes plus or less formally structured: *loose,* on *treasure hunts,* like *inquests* or *web quest.* A basic fact to remember is that given the ease of manipulating information digital motion, especially through *cut* and *paste resources,* is essential generate slogans that ensure a work of elaboration about the information.

The search and the selection can be carried out progressively by the same as-students, with the guidance of the teacher, until they reach the highest degrees of autonomy and possible self-regulation. For example, through the method of learning by projection cough. What's more, is important what the students understand by what is necessary evaluatethe information found. TO leave from there, not only teach them to to work with informationcoming from different sources, otherwise as well, guide them for plan excuse me communicateand share the results and, fundamentally, act based on ethics and responsibility.Reliability in the use of information.

Finally, we must remember that although the development of these skills is essential, ties, so is teaching them in a framework of activities that makes sense, that is significant and relevant.

Some criteria for evaluate the information

Necessarily we will have what to invest weather on rank, to select and discriminate.AND, also teach how it do.

The evaluation of the materials that are available on the Network sometimes requires having Lots of knowledge of the area. However, when you do not have this knowledge, estimate Credibility involves asking yourself a few questions:

Who: who are the sources of information? Does the name of the organization appear? Organization that publishes and that of the person in charge? Do they provide a contact address? Many times we found this information in "About us" or "Who we are".

When: refers to the validity and updating of the information published.

Why: what are the explicit objectives of the organization? This information it usually appears in "Our mission" or in "Institutional".

Why has the information been published: to sell? To inform with facts and data? For share, put available ideas, knowledge? To parody?

How: refers, on the one hand, to the quality and accuracy of the content (are the sources?, are links provided?, etc.). On the other hand, graphic design and an-veg.

Whose it recommended and excuse me we arrived to East site: the links from and toward a resource they imply a reciprocal transfer of credibility. When a person provides a *link* to another or mentions it, we assume that it works as a recommendation. Bur- bulbs and Callister (2001: 66) state:

"The chain of links that is the Internet is an enormous network of relations of credibility: those who establish active links of trustworthy information and whose information or views are both identified and recognized Mentioned by others, they gain credibility both as users and as information providers. We call this network *a credit system. Ability distributed*".

East It represents one from the methods plus efficient and increasingly plus used for the search of information. The interesting thing about all this is not only the possibility of near identified some sites what us indicate the route toward the resources what us they can result tools, otherwise as well propose to the students the challenge from be providers of information or creators of content and generators of exchange networks. Is In other words, we have opportunities here to offer you a *genuine task* from which learn, and a concrete way to *become visible* and have the first experiences of participation in public life.

Take from decisions on the access to the information
Until the appearance from the media from communication and the TIC on the education, the question by the reliability from a source no was raised what a need. The contents and the shape on what East was submitted on the book from text they rested, fundamentally, on the credibility of the publisher. It has not been usual in the classrooms to practice questions question the intentions of the authors or the treatment they made of the different themes. Manuel Area Moreira (2002b), specialist on new technologies and education, He says:

"The book from text is the principal material what has the faculty wherecontent is provided and the prescriptions are operationalized on a practical level. toons of a specific curricular program. As Gideon suggests, the school texts are the translator resources and mediators between the pro- official implementation of the curriculum and classroom practice. In the text is the methodology that enables the development of the objectives, are Once the contents have been selected and sequenced, a group ofactivities on them, the teaching strategy is implicit.acne what the teacher should follow.

But, on the other hand, with the greater volume of information we have at our disposal more number of sources. The characteristic is that they are scattered, they appear in different all formats, styles and designs; serve various purposes, and have not always been created specifically for educational purposes.

With the incorporation from the information and the resources from the TIC I know make necessary vole-to ask ourselves, with regard to this issue, what resources we will use, how we will combine them, if we are going to provide all the information that we consider important. Important or we are going to encourage in the students the practice of searching and reflection. We consider that these alternatives they are not exclusive.

Web 2.0
We are entering a new stage of the Internet, which has been given a name: Web 2.0. This is the term used to refer to a new generation of applications. Toons and systems from the Web what allow set up relations from many-to-manyor communities. The Web 2.0 It represents a change from conception from the Net. TO differ-of the previous one, with static websites, rarely updated and without interaction with the Username, the Web 2.0 is a platform collaborative where I know create contents dynamically, that is, they are produced on the network and can be edited on the spot. This is possible Thank you to tools what require very few knowledge technicalcos. By example, from the encyclopedias *on-line* we passed to the concept from the Wikipedia, onwhich anyone can participate in the development of the themes; of the sites personal to weblogs, much easier to publish and update; of directories to organize content, to those of *tagging* or social labeling, in which the categorization toing from that published is done by the themselves users. From East mode, the Webhappens to be a platform before what a means, medium or

channel from communication.

The proposal of the creators and developers of Web 2.0 is to permanently improve mindfully this new architecture of participation where you read, listen or watch, it is done by sharing, socializing, collaborating and, above all, creating. Here the innovation arises from features distributed by developers independent andthe change is permanent. The conception is that "Web 2.0 is not exactly a technology, but the attitude with which we must work to develop on the Internet. The only constant should be the change, and on Internet, the change should from be Presentplus frequently".

Some Applications and systems from theWeb 2.0

Podcast: Audio file distributed through an RSS file. In the project collaborative podcast.org (on Spanish: http://www.podcast-es.org/) I know condense everything it regarding this resource: an exhaustive list of podcasts, information on how to make them, programs.

You Tube.com: stores videos and it allows, using the code HTML, his republication. East harmless code allowed to millions from blogging and publications electronics, insert videos stored on youtube.com on their own publications. The republished acquires for free and simply the ability to transform automatically his publication on multimedia and interactive. For the distributor original (by example You Tube.com), the republication it means increase significantly his surface from Contact with user's potentials on him _

Competencies basic: learn to search for information, to learnand to take part According Carless Monroe (2005), the competencies for search for information and learnto learn I know refer to the set from strategies what allow learn to leave from their

Own resources. These aim to train an apprentice:

Permanent, capable from learn to it length from all his lifetime and from adapt to the changes;

Autonomous that uses its resources in a self-directed way. That is, someone capable to internalize guidelines, recommendations and guides from other more expert and that somehow way they accompany him;

Strategic, what dispose from resources and from knowledge on function the target per-Following, and make context-aware decisions Learning;

What *self-regulate* (supervise, monitor) his process from learning, take decisionsregarding what, how, when and where to learn at each moment;

What learn from situations from teaching no formal (museums, programs from televisionson, newspapers, etc.).

The development of civic competences, on the other hand, focuses its interest on the con- along with knowledge, skills and dispositions to contribute to coexistence, participate democratically in public life and value pluralism in the pursuit the well common. The integration from the TIC offers opportunities and tools powerful-sass to form citizens:

Informed and with a critical view, based on the reflection and the argumentation;

With a attitude open to the dialogue and respectful from the diversity;

What participate on shape active and responsible on the lifetime public?

TheICT as an object of study? Developing critical capacity
We have differentiated *information* from *knowledge* and presented some criteria for evaluate the information. As we saw, these are two important actions since it has been lying to assimilate the two concepts and as well I know ha overrated the availability byabove the quality of the information. Despite taking all possible precautions on the evaluation from the reliability from the information, yet we run the risk from get-view the Internet as a neutral source of information or simply as a help or resource pedagogical. Is important pose issues about from the interests from the authors and fromthe shapes from representation the world what this information diffuse. Is say, what his-suggests David Buckingham (2005) – researcher and specialist in media education–,the TIC must be incorporated what object from study to the side from others media what themovies, television and radio.

One of the aims of education points to the development of critical capacity. But of what is meant when the term "critical" is used? What differentiates a critical approach of an uncritical one? Who defines what is uncritical?

Buckingham says that the prevailing approach to media education is associated "criticism" to *demystify,* to *demythologize,* to make ideology visible and alert on the limitations from the texts media. This position is conceived on termspurely negatives already what his target is mark the deficiencies from the media (Blackberry-them, ideological, aesthetic), and It seems to imply assume from right now some type from censorship.

What's more, on the practice I know produces to often a situation on the what only I know lendattention to *a* reading truly review, what curiously tends to be or coincidewith the teacher's reading. When students understand that this is the orientation toing what taking the job on media and TIC, infer what to accuse the limitations from the media is the answer what I know waiting from they. Buckingham holds what already to leave from theten years old, children tend to be very good at identifying these *deficiencies* in educational programs. The television and what I know show critics to the respect. Under East focus and Dadaist the easewith which the students grasp that this is what has to be done, can lead to in a situation where the teacher strives to teach students things that they believe what already they know. By East reason, Buckingham holds what I know they need shapesanalyzes that do not depend on making "correct" readings.

35 For this, the development of critical thinking skills is sustained when there is room for what is personal, to the to share interpretations, answers and feelings subjective; to describedaily experiences with the media and reflect on them. It is about promoting a more analytical and reflective vision, trying to situate it within an understanding more spacious. Likewise, it is necessary to structure the time and energy involved in theteaching critical thinking. That is, to adopt a work rhythm that allows the student develop their thinking, allocate time to reflection, to questioningto the experimentation of alternative solutions in problem solving, to the job evaluation, etc. It is also very important to teach the transference of skills of critical thinking to other situations and other contexts.

Teaching critical thinking skills is not just about analyzing the construction of the logic of the argument, but also how the meaning is constructed through from the combination from the images and the texts, the perception from *it what I know maybe*

Say from the reading of the gestures, the conjectures about *the unsaid,* etc. other else- Something to keep in mind is what Roger Cartier (2000) points out:

"The books electronics organize from way new the relationship Come in the let's-toon and the acts, the organization and the argumentation, and the criteria from theproof. Write or read on is new species from book supposed break off fromthe attitudes usual and transform the techniques from accreditation the speech wise, I I mean to the appointment, the note to the foot from page [...] Every a from are shapesfrom try out the validity from a analysis I know find deeply modifiedfrom what the Author can develop his argumentation according a logic what nois necessarily linear or deductive, otherwise open and relational, where the reader can Consult by he same the documents (records, images, words, music) what They are the objects or the instruments from the research. On Eastsense, the revolution from the modalities from production and from transmission from texts is as well a mutation epistemological fundamental".

Until here we have considered different elements for approach the teaching the thought critic within critical analysis and criticism as a literary genre. Now Burbles' andCallister (2001: 62) I know they ask what type from access to the TIC okay the pain have, and they answer:

"It is necessary to focus attention on the ability of users to choose,evaluate and analyze what they find there [on the Internet]. An efficient access supposed the ability and the Will from to select and evaluate the immense dog-amount of material available and also the ability to be heard and seen, contribute with good information, ideas and points of view own".

This us talks from complement the *analysis* with the *production* on the job with media andTIC. Production what I know strengthens with the ease from to post what us contributes the Web 2.0 andthe possibility from to earn presence on Internet being a supplier credible from information. When I know gives to the student's opportunities for produce, the most from the times give bill from understandings sophisticated. How much better known create contents (photo novels, weblog, video, etc.), better will be able evaluate the resources from others and appreciate the good ones designs and the Applications imaginative; will be able distinguish elements superficial from the important for form independent opinions about the value and quality of the information, etc. Ade- plus, they themselves perceive a value aggregate on the learning when perform job spractical, interact with others and they play with the shapes and conventions from the media and from Internet. By other side, yes we combine this, by example, with a job on the information from actuality [36,] including different formats and media, we will be contributing to develop- call the competencies citizens. What indicate bubbles and Callister (2001: 70):

"What is at stake here is not just education. [...] also has to watch with the opportunities labor, the acquisition from resources cultural and of entertainment, social interactions and, increasingly, information and political participation".

With all the elements developed so far in this material, it seems clear that the growth from the skills the thought critical should hold on from a mode plus

General, and no restrict to the media from communication or TIC. The thought critical is an attitude, a provision what search *fissures walkable* on the knowledge, problematize, be on *condition from alert.* To teach the skills the thought critical it implies what the students acquire knowledge and, as well, make them understand what from the approach scientific They are provisional, what suppose a inevitable cutout and what on the ambit from the Sciences I know produce encounters and clashes from theories. Obviously, what teachers must handle is tension and the necessary gradualness from the teaching from these topics and issues. No let's forget what the ability review it implies no give nothing by sitting and assume the confusion, the doubt, but as well the curiosity and the astonishment.

Third key:
Others shapes from organize the information, from represent and from narrate. It audiovisual, it multimedia and it hypermedia

"The rationality I know league to everyone those lofts, basements and ins and outs from the mind, until now careless, where cavort the emotions, the metaphors and the imagine-nation". Kieran Egan, *The imagination on the teaching and the learning.*

The mass media have played and continue to play a prominent role and rise in the configuration of lifestyles, values, fashions, customs, attitudes and opinions.

TO through from the media I know they have wrought levels from aspiration, Models from ide-certification and from participation on the sphere public, and a new countryside from knowledge on turnstilefashionable and current. Television, especially, provides us with many themesto converse in everyday life. Added to this scenario are ICTs and the speed with whichthat adolescents tend to adopt new devices and services [37]. As I said- mos in the line "The important thing is the chip, Mabuchi", generational gaps are opened on the relationship with the technologies and I know they invest the roles on the to teach and the learn. By other side, to the classical intermediation from the books and the teachers on the access to the cone-foundation and the information, I know sum the relationship direct what the student can have with the sources, their diversity and their multimedia and hypertext forms. All this togetherto the transformations that we mention in the different strokes, is what has contributeddo to to form a "new climate cognitive and from learning" [38,] on the what I know mess up

Sequences and hierarchies, and on the what the Adults feel to have lost the control on thecontents to the access children and youths. The side from the institution school, this I knowtranslate on the decrease from his influence cultural and ideological on the training from thechildhood and the youth; this is, on others words, the "lost from his hegemony socialize-dory". [39] According the Professor Tomasz Tadeu gives Silva (1998: 10), "the institution officiallyin charge from the homework from transmission cultural condense the space from the crisis what I know shape on the confrontation from it old with it new". According the Author, the dimension cultural from the crisis from the school I know Explain what the difficulty from reorganize around from a Pattern cultural differentthe from the modernity what you it gave origin and the structured during the century XX.

We have already seen that although ICTs bring about significant changes in what refers to the production, storage and circulation of information, the transfers substantive formations of our time occur in the forms of perception and in the strategies of thought, production and acquisition of knowledge on the one hand, and, on the other, in the approach of contemporary problems from new areas of research, the blurring of disciplinary boundaries, the inseparability from the science and the ethics and from changes on the conceptions, beginning and procedures frommany scientific fields. Understanding this allows us to put the differences into perspective. Come in the practices everyday around from the media and the new technologies and the park-tics own from the institution school. Many times, so much on the literature specializedas in the perceptions of the actors involved, the school-media relationscommunication or school-ICT and teachers-young people are presented as relations of opposition position, in which differences are polarized. The dichotomy boils down to associating the teachers, the school and the culture written, faced to the youths, the media, the TIC and audiovisual and digital culture. Although there is usually tension, the approach from complexity, and not from simplification, allows us to recognize the dimensions and relocate the integration of ICTs in schools within the framework of the epistemological revolution contemporary myology, of the problem of change. Necessarily, the arrival of the media audiovisual and the TIC it implies *reorganize* time, spaces, routines, content- two, and ways of approaching knowledge. It is about gathering and combining to *integrate* the *old* technologies (blackboard, chalk, books, notebooks and pens) to the *new ones* with the end from what arise a model better. TO through from the integration from media and the varietyof languages seeks to prepare young people not only to understand and interpret the images (in general), but also to build knowledge in other ways. We're speaking from diverse shapes from known, learn and represent, from classrooms mule-sensorial and dynamic that allow a greater interaction between the teacher and the students, and among students.

Another step to take in the direction of the "reform of thought", as Mo- rim, is to understand the complementation of sensitivity and reason. Jerome Bruner (1997: 31), from the psycho-cultural perspective states: "there is no doubt that emotions and feelings are represented in the processes of creating meaning and in our constructions of reality. The addition of media audiovisual and ICT facilitates this task because it involves working on other logics: what affective, the sensitivity, the body. The image What source from information, What modeof knowing, implies enhancing the facets of mental activity such as analogy, intuition, global thinking, synthesis, all processes associated with the right hemisphere.right. Is important emphasize are ideas: We speak from *to integrate* resources, tools,hemispheres, reason and intuition, and no from *replace* a logic by other neither machines by
people. And to do it with flexibility, because "each mind is different from the others and is a perspective different about the world [...] How much higher be the flexibility withthat we conceive how things could be, richer, newer and more

efficient it will be the senses that we compose". Kieran Egan (1999: 28-31 and 107), professor at Education and author of these lines, says that the development of the imagination is decisive for the development of rationality. For him, "a conception of rationality that does not sees the imagination as its 'antenna' is sterile". We already raised it: knowledge that which is in our memory is accessible to the action of the imagination; we can only build up worlds possible, this is conceive excuse me could be the stuff, from it what alreadywe know.

The logic of working with ICT also invites students to a collective process and characterized by having a *productive purpose* : a "work", which involves tasks that must be taught formally, such as the design of ideas, the investigation of topics, the planning of the activities, the preparation of the experience, the exercise collective product construction. Here we speak, on the one hand, of interaction in a space where students help each other, each according to their skills, and where the teacher facilitates and encourages the learners to "scaffold" each other too. Collective works, according to Bruner (1997: 41), have the characteristic of producing and sustaining group solidarity, because "they create in the group forms *shared* and *negotiable* from to think". [40] By other, produce plays it implies "outsource",and with it get "a *record* from our efforts mental, a record what is 'was-of us' […] that materializes our thoughts and intentions in a way more accessible to reflective efforts" (Bruner, 1997: 42). The works are the forms thought materials. The mere fact of producing them implies a job of putting test, reflection, evaluation, reformulation, research, exchange and negotiation, from opening to looks different and, to the time, from assumption from a pointof sight. Some will do them in more conscious and committed ways, others will not. So much. By that is important give them the chance from reflect on the process, "pro- drive metacognitions on the construction site" and generalize, to leave from the experience, with you lookto future situations. It is as we stated in the previous key: there are certain types of understanding that are fully attained only through the experience of the production.

Substantive transformations around knowledge and disciplines; opening to other type from knowledge related with the body and the sensitivity; the chance from pro-produce works; All of these are central issues to take into account when working with ICT.In the classroom.

In the following sections we will delve into some particularities of the forms of organize the information, from represent and from narrate what introduce the modes audiovisual-them, multimedia and hypertext. In addition, we will highlight some of the possibilities from learning what, what educators, us interested promote. We will start analyzing separately elements of orality and the visual, already present in teaching, and signs we will see how they are reconfigured by incorporating ICT. Finally, we will present the skills associated with these aspects of the media and new technologies that is need to develop: learn to communicate now to collaborate.

The orality

Orality is a constitutive element of relationships and exchanges in life every day. The conversations, the stories, the songs, the radio they are some from the insdances of exchange and oral transmission. We can also mention the importance from music for young people and for the construction of identities.

Orality is also a constitutive element of school practices. The order- birth space the classroom -the provision from the banks and blackboards– provides the conditions of an organization of speech and silence. For example, banks lined up one behind the other facing the blackboard and the teacher indicate the centrality spatial and symbolic of this, who organizes the speaking turns. We see, too, that provide the banks from way what the students form little ones groups or a circle great among all implies a different proposal of speech and exchange.

The voice the teacher follow being a important means, medium from transmission the knowledge. Let us think, for example, in the university and training environment (congresses, dissertations, toons, panels, conferences). This orality [41] has characteristics similar to those own from the societies without writing on how much to his mysticism from the participation, the felt- do community, his concentration on the Present and even the job from formulas. But I know It deals with a more formal orality, based on the use of writing, of printed material and even of TIC.

Orality is not only the space where the auditory predominates, but where it is put into I play the body and the skills for reading the non-verbal. for the specialist in communication and culture Anibal Ford (1994: 37), "orality, narration, co-nonverbal communication are in itself and in its conflicts and relationships with writing and argumentation, at the center of the processes of construction of meaning of our culture. true". We are in a culture where narrating, remembering through narratives, exercising and assess the perception no verbal, to argue to through from the action and the case for perceivethe reality with the body have a strong weight. From agreement with Martin Barber and GermanKing (1999):

"What we need to think about is the deep rapport – the complicity it and complexity of relationships – that today occurs in Latin America between the *orality* that endures as the primary cultural experience of the majorities and technological *visually* , that form of "secondary orality" what weave and organize the grammars techno perceptive from the radio and the movies,of video and television. Well, that complicity between orality and visuallydoes not refer to the exoticism of a Third World illiteracy but to the persistence from strata deep from the memory and the mentality collectivebrought to the surface by the sudden alterations of the traditional fabric that the modernizing acceleration itself entails".

So, we can perceive the cultural density of orality and narration and take itWhat frame for his Recovery What model cognitive on the proposals from teach-whoa For Bruner, the narration is a shape from thought and a vehicle for the creationfrom meaning essential on the Constitution from the subjects. According East Author, "the skill

to build narratives and to understand narratives is crucial in the construction of our lives and the construction of a 'place' for ourselves in the possible world by that we will face". Such is the importance that Bruner gives to work with narration, what summarizes:

"An education system must help those who grow up in a culture to find an identity within that culture. Without it, they stumble in theirefforts to achieve meaning. Only in a narrative mode timely one can build an identity and find a place in the culture own. The schools must cultivate it, nurture her, let from give it by of course".

Egan (1999: 107) comments: "in education we have given pride of place to the concept decontextualized, and It seems what we have forgotten make weather it what the media from co-ammunition plus powerful from our history cultural put from manifest with clarity: what the image affective is decisive on the communication the sense and from the significance".

Remains So outlined the relationship Come in education, orality and narrative for can introduce-circle some lines of work with TIC.

The different media from record sonorous (recorders from Audio, video, CD and DVD) intro-duce interesting opportunities in the dynamics of the oral in the school. can be use digital voice recorders, music and sounds to bring closer students to:

•   techniques of scientific observation, collection and analysis of information: capture of sounds or noises (from a ecosystem, from a environment urban or from animals, by example),for then display and explain them;

•   the record from testimonials oral, to through from interviews, on the frame from researchin the area of social sciences;

•   The production from contents digital oral what can diffuse on Internet. By Ahem- plot, the presentation, Explanation and debate from news the month relative to different areas: archaeological finds, climatic phenomena, environmental issues, politics, scientists, social, etc. I know can, So, point to the deepening from a theme treaty onthe classroom, to through from the execution from a interview to a professional specialized on the area, a poll, a debate, etc., with the motivation from spread it by Internet or visual ^{42} _

The century XX is unthinkable without the paper structural and constitutive played by the imagesfrom the iconography scientific, from the Photography, the movies, from the television, from the advertising andfrom the new digital media.

Any reflection on any means of expression (written texts; personal reports) journalistic, navigation logs; graphic, cartographic, pictorial representations; photography, cinema, etc.) the fundamental question of the specific relationship that exists between the external referent and the message produced by that medium. Is about the matter of *modes of representation.*

In relation to photography specifically, we can say that there is a kind of consensus respect from what the real document photographic *yield bill faithful the man-do* . The credibility enjoyed by the photographic image rests mainly on the conscience what I know have the process mechanic from production from this image. The photographyFaith, before common sense, *cannot lie.* The photo is perceived as a kind of proof that undoubtedly attests to the existence of what it shows. The need for *watch for to believe* I know find there satisfied. It what we see on a Photography is *truth,* afragment of reality, something that exists or has existed before the camera lens. Thejournalistic photography is a document whose veracity we will not doubt a priori.Without embargo, his value documentary film, testimonial, I know presents on the present on a doubleplay: by a side, anyone what have a camera can to register eventsand send them to newspaper Internet sites. And on the other hand, it is easy, thanks to the digitization, retouching and tricking the image.

We are interested in emphasizing that this is not new and for this it is necessary to register this double play on a plot cultural and Social. Will, then, a route historical boundedby the different positions held by critics and theoreticians of photography regarding from East beginning from reality. [43] We will see what in view of the diffusion Social from new technologiesdynamics similar to those we can see today develop. Among them, the feelings found forehead to the perception from the changes, and the needto reorder the cultural and social space.

The Photography what mirror or What transformation from it real?

Photography as a mirror of reality began to arise as an idea from the beginning of the 19th century. Statements (for, against, contradictory, controversial, infuriating) naps) on the Photography they shared the conception from what is, on comparison with thepainting, was *the imitation plus perfect from the reality.* This ability mimetic the obtainedof the very technical nature of the procedure, which was considered to bring out the image *automatically, objectively,* almost *naturally,* without the intervention *of the hand of the artist.* At that time, the social perception was that the technical mutation was enormous, andthis woke up fear and fascination to the time. There was, as well, visions optimists what EC-worked the release the art from the functions social and utilitarian's until that momentexercised by the painting, what to leave from then would take by the Photography. On thistime of change of roles, something occurred that today we would define as *reconversion of the professions:* ancient portrait painters they passed to be photographers. Is What Yes in view of a new?

Technology its acceptance depended on clarifying its areas of concern. In that then, the paper from the Photography consisted on keep the footprints the past and to helpthe sciences in their effort to better understand the reality of the world. Its function was documentary film, from reference, from record and extension from the possibilities from the lookhuman. It was considered *an assistant to memory* or the *simple testimony of what has happened.been.* The art, it imaginary and the creation remained reserved for the painting. I know opposed,So, the *neutrality the apparatus* to the *product subjective of the sensitivity the artist.*

Two centuries then us we asked by what so much then What today is so important establish or set action spaces for emerging technologies. Is it a way of rearrange and give place to it new? Is a shape from resistance in view of the change? Isthe expression of a power struggle for the symbolic and cultural space and for the differencesocial citation?

Photography as a transformation of reality is the idea that appears strongly in the century XX. I know warns what the Photo is eminently coded. From the psychologyperception and analysis of an ideological type, it is argued that the similarity with the reality is a social convention, an arbitrary, cultural, ideological creation. Of this way, it cannot be considered as a mirror because it supposes transposition, analysis, interpretation, even, transformation from it real. By then? On beginning, because offersa image determined by the angle from vision, the distance with respect to the object andthe framing. There is an *eye* that selects what can be photographed and makes decisions. From a analysis ideological I know discuss the pretended neutrality from the camera and the objectivity, since it expresses a particular conception of space: the Renaissance perspective. Ade- Furthermore, the meaning of photographic messages is culturally constructed, not imposes as evidence for every receiver: certain codes of reading. With this, the value of a mirror, of an exact document, of similarity, is questioned. Infallible. Then, by plus faithful what be a image for to transmit information visual, the process from selection forever will reveal the interpretation what his Author is done from itwhat consider relevant.

On the present the Photography I know uses with diverse ends: scientists, journalistic, do- commensals, expressive –artistic, personal–, relatives, legal, illustrative, etc.

His interpretation is a skill important for learn, so what know the sale-ha and limitations the instrument. On the school, to the produce and use Photographs, areconsiderations must be taught. Is important to know from what modes I know they usein the sciences and the arts. For example, in biology, photographic and imaging cameras video serving what helpers for the observation, the record and the documentation. Onteaching, microscopy is widely used in the absence of observation instruments sophisticated. In the area of social sciences, although they are used as testimony or document, exists simultaneously a species from *condition from alert* on the point from viewvoiced by the photographer. The use intensive from the Photographs on the press written for acme- diaper the texts ha deepened the need from no to lose from view are issues.

Considering the documentary possibilities and the characteristic of being crossed bycodes, we present below some lines of work to use the camerasdigital:

• Exploration the instrument. Experimentation from codes. Analysis from the photos. Exercise-citation on different settings and angles from camera with the end from produce a messageconcrete for a addressee defined. On general, on the first essays I know produce

Mistakes basics, on the sense from what the photos no I know correspond with it what I know triedor what they were thought to be.

• Post-production from the image photographic. Yes I know bill with a Program from edition fromimages, you can experiment with different types of *retouching*. From there, discuss on the documentary value, the dissemination of these practices in entertainment magazinesand advertisements, ethical considerations, etc.

I know can use the cameras as support of the scientific observation:

- Capturing images at different times that mark a sequence in the phenomenon studied, for example in the area of biology, the germination of a dicotyledonous seed, the incubation of an egg, the change in the trees of according to the seasons of the year, the fermentation of milk, etc.

-   Capture and record from images illustrative, by example, during a experiment-to (a reaction chemistry "visible" - change from Color, production from gas, etc.- atitration, crystal growth, etc.).

These are just some of the possible approaches. What others imagine? Which peopleor resources documentaries could be consulted for enlarge the perspective and to help todevelop new ideas?

The schemes
On the pulled apart previous we speak from modes from represent and we develop the case fromphotography in relation to the degree of resemblance to what it represents. Now, we will think about the pictures in different levels of abstraction.

Schematization consists of an action of progressive reduction of the complexity from the phenomena and, reciprocally, a increase progressive from the information visual". [44] Visual information is an abstraction and conceptualization operation that is crystallizes in a graphic scheme. In this operation, certain types of information are filtered. Toing from it real and I know encode from a mode plus net and simplified alone the featureswho are interested. The anatomical drawings of Leonardo da Vinci are early examples.Us from the deliberate suppression of certain features for the sake of conceptual clarity. Maps also have this feature of abstraction.

It should be remembered that this type of images has been used in teaching since the very origins of modern educational systems. *Orbits sensualium pectus* or *The world sensitive on images,* the thinker Moravian John Amos Comenius (Hersey brood,1592 - Amsterdam, 1670), is the first illustrated book for educational purposes. In a pro-post, Johann Heinrich Pestalozzi emphasizes the importance of using objects natural on the teaching with the end from achieve the knowledge from the stuff by the stuffthemselves. However, it accepts the use of sheets or models that replace nature. ral. At that time it was thought that there was no essential cognitive difference betweenimage drawn on paper and the visual image of the real object, since both ways it came to mind as representation. Objects and images, as a replacement pictorial from the objects, fulfilled, so, a paper central on the growth from the faculties

Mental, because represented the origin authentic from everything knowledge real. Withoutembargo, the most uses recent indicate a target change:

"The images remained involved in the classroom. But Mom- Mostly, as informative support, 'testimony' of the task or indicator ofrules or events. That was not the hierarchy they had for three centuries.His mission was different. Without a theory to back them up, they remain asa means, medium assistant for provide data the world to study or cooperate on theclass organization. The graphic image, as it is mostly used, mind, no would already 'the object' what would cause the representation on the spiritor the mind when the terms no would allow or they will advise the Contactdirect. The image, now, serves as a text to provide information,to support information of another type or organize information [...]. Four. Five

Nowadays,

[...] at school new discursive forms appear: encyclopedias, books, magazines and newspapers come to play an important place and carry new images from a type and a value very different to the what characterizedto the school boards. The school board, which could be described as 'decontextualized reality', is diluted with the entry of 'reality' and 'theknowledge' via supports no schooled initially (photos, films,and Computer programs)". [46]

Other type from outlining they are the graphics or diagrams what show relations whatoriginally no they are visuals, otherwise temporary or logical. An example is the tree gene-logical, one from the maps relational plus ancient what we know, where a relationshipwhat we could explain what "is the woman from a cousin second from me mother adoptive"can be seen quickly. Whatever the connection, the diagram will put before us eyes what a verbal description could represent with a chain of statements. In this sense, the schematization starts from abstract elements (concepts, data, processes, etc.) to produce the visual information.

On education, the schemes They are acquaintances as well What *organizers graphics*. Are tool-while visuals us allow show regularities, relations, alternatives from action; to exhibit data and processes; describe objects and places; establish relationships between ideas; summarize, facilitateinterpret and understand information. Some of the most used are: paintings synoptic, diagrams, flow charts, time lines, concept maps, networks, etc. One ofThe most important criteria for deciding which type of graphic organizer to use is to define themode from representation on function from the homework cognitive: Yes the homework is understand a causalityor comparison, the design visual should contribute to show it with clarity.

It multimedia

Exist many definitions from multimedia. The finished "multimedia" I know used already beforefrom the computer. I know employed for describe productions what integrated projectorsfrom slides, monitors from video, engravers from Audio, projectors from movies, Come in

Others, for get certain effects through the combination from images and sounds. As well has been used on relationship with programs from education to distance or from teachingfrom Languages what included different media from transmission what radio, television, etc. From therethe Name "Program multimedia". Other meaning the we find on the "packages multi-half" for the teaching. The "package" included materials printed with text and images,ribbons from Audio, video cassettes. To the diffuse the computer personal, starts to talk to each other from "computing multimedia" What a tried from to combine the media audiovisual with texts and Photographs for create a new means, medium on the screen from the computer.

The most important characteristics are: the presence of more than two media or morph- ology's of information (texts, slides, photos, videos, graphics, audio, etc.), and the interconnection, combination and integration of these means. The end result is not sum of each, but a totally new product.

In this module, we will only mention the use of presentation makers or editors.These They are programs computer scientists what inherited some from the features and applications what in view of-recently They had the slideshow or transparencies. From done, I know uses the finished "slide ", on time from pages, for name to the units what make up a presentation. A fromthe advantages from the programs from presentations is what allow insert on the slideshowdifferent *objects* , such What texts, images, graphics, material sonorous, music and evensequences filmic. TO every *object* they can apply to it, what's more, effects from animation.

Presentations are a special type of document, with their own characteristics. A presentation slide is not a page of a book in which you write and write. Guetta with luxury of details. Presentations are used to display information about short and direct way. This implies a great work of synthesis on the part of those who elaborates, to summarize and expose only the necessary data. It also involves work of selection of the graphic material that will accompany the information.

It is important to define the context in which the presentation will be read. Will the former accompanyposition of a speaker? Will it be distributed or shared through Internet?

The presentations they can be from two types: linear or interactive. The first they are those whose slideshow I know happen on a order unique and preset from the first until thelast. They are used for accompany or complement a exposition oral on a themedetermined. The interactive They are those on what is possible to choose which one is the information what I know want watch; the reader from the presentation the he touring by means, medium from links, as if were browsing on Internet. From is shape, every reader can do a route fromreading own self, from agreement to their interests. Carry out East type from presentations is possible Thank you to the ability from to elaborate hyperlinks Come in the different slideshow.

The proposal to include the realization of a multimedia project (with a preview editor)sittings) by part from the students for learn on a determined contentsshould contemplate, in the first place, the proposal of a specific purpose in which the information acquire sense. Is say, on time from generate a *compilation illustrated* ,the homework shall apply for what interpret, explain, apply While expose his pointof sight. This interpretive process requires deciding how to represent the information (with texts, graphics, photos, and videos, audio). For example, they can propose solutions to a specific problem, make a report for a congress or to be presented before a municipal authority, etc. Next, students should be encouraged to:

• take decisions about the type from information necessary for support the solutions

That they got. If there is only one correct answer, if they are not required to be selective, the exercise can become on a exercise from cut and paste. The students must to access to the information, transform it and translate the four provide reasons solid- you give what sustain the contents and the organization from their products multimedia.

- Find and collect the most important information and interpret it in the medium that they are using.

- Order the ideas, the divide on topics plus reduced for every slide; define therelationship Come in are, his organization and sequence; choose the top images for to illustrate the point what want mark. East process contributes to understandings different the theme.

- Analyze the shapes from complement the slideshow with the use from spreadsheets from calculationfor record and illustrate graphically the collected data.

- Introduce complexity with non-linear structures (interactive presentations) thatallow organize different reading tours.

The utilization from these programs It allows the practice from techniques from report, divulgationinformation and advanced communication. They are tools that can be used to develop documents, catalogs or multimedia exhibitions (with photos, *collages,*videos, MP3 files, etc.). We are talking, then, about the use of *systems more physical support* to represent, of different ways, knowledge.

Hypertext, hypermedia

Hypertext is a computer-based structure for organizing information, which make possible the Connection electronics from units textual to through from links inside thesame document or with documents external. [47] hypermedia would the combination from
Hypertext with multimedia. The Web would have, according is definition, a Format hyper me-day, although not everything that is published there has these characteristics.

TO weigh from what the difference Come in are definitions is clear, on the practice, the term-my hypertext has been generalized with great force being used indistinctly both to refer to hypertext in the strict sense as multimedia hypertext – that is, hypermedia– since there are practically no longer hypertexts made up of a single text. call.

Some features:

Not all digitized text is a hypertext, since it consists of links between elements. Internal or external elements. When the link wraps around itself, we have a bounded or limited hypertext (such as CD-ROMs). When it is external, we have ashorizon the Entire website.

•   There are different degrees from linearity on the hypertexts. By a side, many hypertextscan be even more rigid than the traditional text itself, forcing us to traverse preordered paths. At the other extreme, the author can make the paths complement or exclude each other and you can jump from one to another by choosing the order of the reading, from way such what the decisions the reader determine the growth from the history(on fiction) or the point of view that has been chosen (in non-fiction).

•   The non-linearity (or non-sequentially) no is a characteristic inherent the hypertextotherwise a possibility organizational. The hypertext have the advantage from to go plus there from the line-quality of most printed texts, without this meaning that such quality is essential, nor that it is impossible to obtain in the printed texts, as evidenced by books like *Hopscotch* by Julio Cordozar (1963) or movies like *Eternal glow of a mind without memories* (2005, directed by Michel Gundry) *Run Lola, run* (1998, directed by Tom Tynker) and *The effect butterfly* (2004, directed by Eric Brass and J. Mac-Key Grubber).

•   Hypertext, from the reader's point of view, is an electronic document in which what the information I know presents on shape from a net from nodes and links. To choose Come in oneor other always implies a previous calculation about what we can find from the other hand, an anticipation that, on the one hand, is cognitive (in relation to what is read) and, on the other, other, have a outcome mechanic, already what I know treats from move the *mouse* and Activate a zonefrom the screen.

- Hypertext, from the point of view of the author or producer, is a writing systembranched that offers a starting point and different paths to travel through its links. The hypertext requires the Author a job additional respect from it what make aAuthor traditionally to the Send material to the printing, because the contents -what's more frombe worked up stylistically and rhetorically- should be organized hyper textually.

Can say, then, what the hyper textuality has features what sue a new understanding the text what I know read and a set different from strategies for the write- true, and by it so much offers a countryside from opportunities for the intervention educational.

No linear -Tabular

Non-linearity is an organizational possibility of hypertext. However, for Christian Vandendorpe (2003), define a finished to leave from a denial or absenceownership is not entirely accurate. To describe the opposition to linearity proposes the term "tabularity", which comes from the French *tableau* (table) and represents an analogy Come in the way on what I know "read" a frame and the reading from a text.

While linearity refers to a series of elements ordered sequentially essentially and essentially dependent on the order of time, tabularity puts manifest the possibility of the reader to "access visual data in the order that he choose, delimiting from entry the sections what you are interested".

With only to think on the diaries and excuse me present the information, can give us account- ta from what the tabularity is quite plus ancient from it what commonly I know believe. Withthe appearance the daily and the press from big chuck, to leave the century XIX, and especiallyafter the appearance of full-page headlines, the text escapes linearity original of the word to present itself in visual blocks that respond and com- complemented on the surface of the page, as if it were a "textual mosaic", according to Marshall McLuhan's metaphor. The layout is "guided not by the logic the speech otherwise by a logic space." "The amount from columns, the typeface- image, the position of the illustrations, the color, thus allow you to zoom in or out, select and disunite units that, in the newspaper, are informative units. The collating pray then What a rhetoric the space what restructure the order the speech(its temporal logic) to reconstitute an original discourse that, precisely, is the speech the daily".

In our time there is no doubt that tabularity corresponds to a requirementfrom organization from the texts from type informative, from way from allow a appropriate-toing so effective What be possible. Unquestionably, his function primary is to hold backthe reader whose attention is unstable or momentary, contrary to that of an organization linear organization, which is directed at a "background reader". But it is also very convenient for the communication of varied information that can be selected according tothe interests.

Seen from this aspect, the printed text no longer depends exclusively on the linear order, but tends to integrate some of the characteristics of a painting swept by the reader's eye in search of significant elements. Thus, this can break away from the text thread to go directly to the relevant item. Therefore, one construction site is call tabular when It allows the deployment on the space and the manifestation simultaneous from various elements what can to serve from help to the reader for identify their joints and find it plus quickly possible the information's what you they interest

According Vandendorpe, the notion from tabularity, what's more from represent a mode inter-not of data disposition, it refers to two realities: the "functional tabularity", expressed by the summaries, the indexes, the division into chapters and paragraphs (means of organizational order that facilitate access to the content of the text); the "tabularity vi- seal", which allows the reader to go from reading the main text to the notes, glosses, figures, illustrations, all present in the double space of the page. This ta- clarity is present in newspapers and magazines, highly developed on the screen (pages web or CD-ROM). To conform to this type of tabularity, the text is worked asa material visual.
Competencies basic: learn to communicate and to to collaborate

I know refers to the set from strategies for can communicate with others to through from devices.

Be able to communicate through the specific language of the discipline.

Use different means to communicate.

- Be capable from learn on shape cooperative and collaborative, it what requires teaching system- mastic and rigorous, well no I know give to spontaneously. Is important achieve the communality from objectives, reciprocity in relationships, interdependence, even in the face of asymmetry of knowledge. I know treats from a job permanent with others forming networks from knowledge.

From inclusion, strokes, keys, opportunities and Projects
To think the TIC What politics from inclusion, reflect on the strokes the world current, read the keys for the integration from the new technologies on the classroom and make us new questions and building positions are part of the purpose of this module. Until Now we have taken the different themes and tried to identify dimensions, perspectives, interpretations. We seek to reflect on the new and change; trace lines continuity and rupture. The "Opportunities to generate appropriation scenarios significant ICT" that we present in the following section will complete a pro- put from integration from the new technologies what contemplate and encourages the reading from the complexity of the world, the cultural, social and political density of the subject, and the contexts action specifics.

Know what others have thought and researched, discuss with the authors, be aware from it what happens -and, to the time, be conscious from what it we make to through from the look from the others and the story they put together–, exchange ideas and opinions with our colleagues, students, friends, etc., helps us to develop positions – personal, theoretical, methodological – and visualize possible futures. We also understand that the perceptions toons of the present change when we look to the future and *project* scenarios from of understanding the forces at play. In this way, these *visits to the future* suppose an intentional reading of the context, a construction of the problem and an intervention proposal. They involve critical and *creative* subjects (Giordano, 2002), able from interpret and produce something new, understanding it "new" What that what introduces components that did not exist before but also as that which modifies and reorganize what exists.

In a broader sense, the *project* represents a central aspect in the process of constitution of the subject, that is, the ability to define a *life project.* To teach it is also part of a life project and, in turn, the school institution -among others– is support and guide of the life project of the new generations. Moreira Area(2001) says: "Our current time is that of the awareness that the future is the responsibilitybility from the we inhabit the Present". On East frame from though, the decisionswhat we take they are forever decisions ethics. AND the decisions ethics they are complex, wellthey do not only involve questions of good and bad. They assume an *integration* of three dimensions: the *rationality* of the objectives –educational, political–, the curriculum and the plannings; sensitivity towards people, what they think, feel , their wishes, their needs, their preferences, his delusion, his discouragement, their aspirations;the perspective that includes the *context* and to *long term* .

From all this material, clear guidelines emerge to generate proposals for teaching with ICT components. These are conceived as a common framework open unfinished and that *will* be specified when it is elaborated with the teachers, in the schools.

As we have been proposing throughout the module, for the integration of ICT in thejob school result necessary reflect on the relationship Come in technology, peopleand knowledge from a perspective complex what integrate it gnoseological, it communitynational, it psychological, it Social and it didactic. On the present, the modes from to accessto the information and to the knowledge They are multiple and varied. The school, then, havesignificant role in teaching systematic processes of discovery, selection, tion, organization, understanding and communication. Hence, the work with ICT in the school should point plus what to the domain purely instrumental from the technology, toits use in a creative and critical way in environments of reflection, debate and learningsignificant.

From this way, the pedagogical integration of ICT means conceiving them:

As a teaching resource and, also, as an object of study and reflection, a means of expression and production, and knowledge management mode, depending on objectives pedagogical

As part of a transversal project, guided by teaching purposes and understanding giving the chance from to pursue ends cultural, social and politicians: building fromidentities, visibility, communication, training and citizen participation.

As components of learning environments, reflection, understanding and communication toing, combinable with other resources, in the different curricular subjects.

The pedagogical integration from ICT is power to:

Alternate instances individual and group from job to through from dynamic collaborative.

Point to the autonomy the student, guided by the teacher, and to the growth from compete- tions for participation in public life: learning to learn, managing information and communicate.

Manage resources, spaces and time from mode flexible and attending to the complexitythe context and of content to teach.

Design the interaction between students in the classroom space and in the virtual.

Handle the diversity from chores on simultaneity and the joint from instances pre-essential and online.

Incorporate questions related to the social and cultural dynamics of the media communication and from the TIC, So What those related with the posts and content-two that are produced there, share and they circulate.

Dialogue with the consumption cultural juveniles and take them what point from departure forthe reflection and construction of new knowledge and productions.

By virtue of all this, ICTs are thought of in contexts of complex appropriation, in those that the use of technology is not a goal in itself but rather responds to objectives pedagogical and purposes from the teaching. We will consider what the use is "okay-when it manages to integrate in a pertinent way the potentialities of the tooland the needs it intends to satisfy, and when the result of the integration processstin could not have been achieved without working with that technology. The incorporation of ICT, from this perspective, aims to promote use with a pedagogical, social and cultural, to add value to the teaching proposals and to offer students, new opportunities for learnings significant and relevant.

Thus, work in accordance with these guidelines implies, on the one hand, knowing the new languages, approaching "new cultures", rethinking teaching strategies, design proposals didactics, try shorten the gaps generational and to consider thesubjective affectation that occurs in the appropriation of media discourse and peda-logical AND, by other, requires the involvement and the job collaborative from the equipmentinstitutional, and the strengthening the role and the authority the teacher on the processes fromconstruction of knowledge about ICT and with

We present below opportunities for the organization and the search for the information and for communication with digital concept maps, web quests and weblog. In each section, after describing these ICTs, we will identify the contributions pedagogical what provide to the job school and the requirements from management by part theteacher.

Opportunities for organizing information to through from maps conceptual digital

The organization from the information is a part important on everything process from building fromknowledge. The updating, fragmentation and invisibility of the contents that circulateon the media audiovisual and digital from communication do what the selection, classify-tin, categorization and hierarchy from data I know come back chores central on the processes fromunderstanding. The planning from any search from information requires schedule the pro-transfer, identify knowledge previous on the theme, set up axes on the what I know aims toenlarge it what I know known or synthesize and to integrate the findings to it what already I know knew.

A shape from develop the capabilities linked with the organization from the inform- tion is to leave from the utilization from organizers graphics. The diagrams, maps or networksconceptual, boards, lines from weather, schedules, and diagrams from flow allow riper- visually lay out the information and graphically capture ideas and concepts. As well they help to develop a complex thought and to reflect on it and communicate it. The different digital tools allow students to organize what they know and, incorporating new concepts to others already learned, proposing preliminary schemes from content, synthesize texts, pose problems in complex form.

Choosing graphic organizers for school work requires identifying both the objectives of the pedagogical proposal and the specificities of each tool. Lie. If what you want, for example, is for students to locate certain events inside from a period from weather determined for what visualize and understand the relationship temporary Come in they, the organizer graphic plus suitable is a line from time-po. By other part, yes it what I know search is what the students understand the relationship Come inconcepts, the most pertinent is a concept map.

Map conceptual digital: synthesis from the tool
A conceptual map is a model of graphic representation of knowledge. His construction supposes an intellectual activity and allows the student to visualize the training what already has acquired and it knew what incorporates, and, from is shape, organize thethoughts for better understanding.

Can be built with pencil and paper. Without embargo, some programs specific from soft-ware allow you to expand your potential. The use of these digital tools simplifies and speeds up the handling, storage, retrieval and multimedia approach of the contents. In this sense, one of the main advantages of working with conventional maps conceptual on computer is what the concepts and the relations they can be modified pluseasily than in paper format, while the different versions of what has beenproduced they can be archived and recovered when the homework it require. By other pair-tee, the digital medium allows to expand the visual potential of the conceptual map by admitting the inclusion of icons, static or animated drawings (gif). From these possibilities medium, then, the transposition from idioms, the revision, the rewrite, the consultation and comparison of previous productions or reflection on processes and changes can give become frequent slogans of integration from ICT in Classroom.

The tools digital allow, by other part, build up maps conceptual with on the- ces or hyperlinks to others resources (photos, images, graphics, videos, texts, pages Web, sounds, other maps concepts, etc.) to expand the explanation of the contents

Or search for related information. Also, since maps can be stored on an Internet or intranet server, they can be worked on collaboratively distance.

The complexification from topics or problems; the search from information extension on a topic of interest; reflection on what is relevant and what is secondary; the design and evaluation tin of navigation structures; reflection on the cultural conventions of representation; the organization of work in complementary task teams and the communication from it produced They are others from the chores to the what contributes the job with these organizers graphics in digital format.

Pedagogical contributions of the work with conceptual maps in Format digital
Favors the job with supports multimedia.

Offers a mode for the externalization the thought and the knowledge constructed.

Gets better the skills from understanding from texts, from organization (classification, cat-ionization and relationship) from the information and from representation the knowledge on shapehyper textual and multimedia.

Facilitates the communication, the exchange from information and the negotiation from mean-two to leave from the building from Models graphics from representation and, from East mode, thedevelopment of shared understanding.

Enables the job collaborative and the building collective from knowledge.

Favors processes from reflection on the own processes from learning.

Developing from the tool
The elements that make up a digital concept map are:

Concepts: abstraction of the characteristics that define an object or event. I know represented graphically within ellipses, circles, or rectangles.

Connectors or *words from link:* I know they use for link the concepts and for indicate thetype of relationship between them. "It is a", "they are characterized by", "it depends of", "produce", etc. are examples of connectors. These are written on or next to the line that joins the concepts (link line).

Propositions: two or more conceptual terms joined by linking words to form a semantic unit. "The city has an industrial area" or "The human being needs oxygen" are examples of propositions.

Multimedia and hypertext resources: photos, videos, sounds, links to pages website etc.

According to the pedagogical objectives, there are multiple strategies to guide students.Students in the construction of concept maps. The starting point can be:

Pose a *question from focus* what direct the job toward a target. The questions,plus what the topics, delimit the contents and focus the resolution from the activities proposals- you. Are questions they can be created so much by the teacher what by the students?

Select the concepts that the teacher wants the students to include in their maps and list them. The aspect that presents the greatest challenge and difficulty in the construction tin of concept maps is the elaboration of propositions. That is, determinewhich linking words will clearly describe the relationship between concepts. Therefore,deliver to the students a ready from concepts no you remove difficulty to the buildingof the map and allows the teacher to detect which concepts the student is not integrating correctly.

To complete the structure from a Map predesigned For topics complex, I know can to optfor giving students a partial map, based on an "expert" map, taken from the bibliography or accomplished by the teacher. There the slogan can be expand it with conceptioncough and more specific relationships. In this case, the initial map acts as a "trigger"and scaffolding for the students. As well, the slogan can be enlarge a concept tothrough a "sub map" (a map that enlarges the detail of the relationships involved insome complex concept).

Then, the students they will have to:

Group the concepts whose relationship is close.

Order them from the most abstract and general to the most concrete and specific.

Represent them and place them on the diagram.

Connect them.

Look for, to select resources multimedia and hyperlinks -from agreement with his mean-activity and relevance–, locate them and add them where appropriate.

Find out the Map, check the relations, look after what no I know have repeated or Super-put concepts.

• Reflect on the Map. Correct, enlarge, put off, change, rebuild, reorganize,establish previously unseen relationships, etc.

The advantage of using a computer to make these maps is that it allows It allows you to easily add or remove elements or relations, change their position, as well as such as adding images or other multimedia resources that help clarify the representation of a theme. In other words, it speeds up the preparation, the refinement process, modification and extension. It is also easy to interconnect and establish cross-relationships between the maps. In addition, they can be "saved" as images and be reused on others jobs, what monographs or presentations. Dadaistthe possibility of being hosted on a server, they can also be built remotely and on collaboratively, and give them to know publicly.

As stated, concept maps are graphic organizers that favor the understanding, illustrate graphically the relations Come in concepts and they help on the learn-new information by clearly showing the integration of each new idea into a existing pool of knowledge.

They are tools for the extraction the meaning from texts and on the job from laboratory andfield. The organization of concept maps allows easy review of the information presented as they help to identify key concepts and relationships. For the building from a Map conceptual, necessarily the students they will have whatto work on the information, for decide Yes is relevant or no for the growth of a theme. With or without the help of the teacher, they will be able to identify which part of the topic they should deepen, review or rethink.

It is important to keep in mind that the use of concept maps in information systems hypertext me multimedia requires to teach to design the hypertext, to to ease the navigate-ton and the reading path of the map, that is, to represent the knowledge of this mode.

The maps they can be elaborate, as well, by the teachers for present the theme to thestudents. Even, Dadaist his ability from contain hyperlinks, they can offer maps digital concepts as a format for students to navigate and search information. They are also used to plan the curriculum, selecting the significant contents and determining which routes are followed to organize the significantfallen. I know can build up a Map global on what appear the ideas plus importantthat will be taken into account during the course, to then move on to more specific ones what group topics or blocks from contents and, finally, to the Map detailed from the class.This will help students to relate in a coordinated way the different levels of work and to fit the details into the framework of global relationships.

Requirements from management by part the teacher
Define at what point in the project and for what pedagogical purpose the resources will be used. Conceptual maps (investigate previous ideas or notions, present a topic or project, propose relationships between disciplines, classify and categorize given information, perform a final synthesis, evaluate the understanding of a topic etc.).

Generate spaces for reflection and awareness of students regarding the co-awareness, uses, meanings and opportunity to use digital maps in the project (reflect and discuss similarities, differences or complementary uses between the tool to to work and others acquaintances, etc.). Is say, what's more from to know excuse me build upa map is important for students to learn to make decisions about when use them and assess whether the conceptual map is the most appropriate procedure for get the proposed goal and solve activity scheduled.

To choose the point from departure for the building from the maps (a question from focus,a Map partial, a ready from concepts, etc.) Then, make explicit the target general, forwork on the contents and key concepts. Take advantage of the tool to approach complex problems from a multiplicity of prospects.

Foresee moments for learn to handle the tool on growing degrees from com-lenity. Promote a flexible and efficient use of time. Take into account the deadlines production work, both individually and in groups.

Propitiate what the students self-regulate and control his own self process from apprentice- heh, relating the knowledge obtained with schemes cognitive previous.

Encourage the creation of learning communities in a climate of trust and cooperation. Encourage the possibility of sharing information and expressing ideas as a way to improve teaching and learning processes. Contemplate the opportunities to generate collaborative dynamics with professors of different subjects.

Provide for the search and organization of multimedia resources, especially due to the Possibility of editing the concept map in hypertext format. Teach to analyze and evaluate the relevance of the selected concepts, of the relationships established between them and the resources used.

Plan the archive of the maps and propose dynamics for their registration and enrichment. I lie throughout the development of a project.

Consider the use of these schemes to monitor and evaluate the process of student learning.

Differences with others tools for the organizationfrom the information
The maps conceptual digital they can be used for the resolution from problems,the outlining from points important to approach and the hierarchy from the Stepsand interrelations. As well, they can be used by the students for approach tothe understanding from a theme or problematic punctual, or well for synthesize the theme-treated cases, to design an investigation, to propose the writing of a work monograph, etc. Timelines, unlike maps, locate graphically the temporary situation of an event or process, evidencing the succession of events and the simultaneity with others events the moment, what even they cancondition

each other.

A from the differences primordial what do to the job with maps conceptual on real-ton with others tools for the organization from the information is the from to incorporate the concept from networks hierarchical from meaning. When we speak from maps conceptual,us we refer to strategies from organization from information, from concepts and, as well, fromtheir relationships.

Given these characteristics, concept maps can complement and integrateI know to a proposal plus wide what include others TIC, What web quests or searches thetreasure, which are strategies for the structured search for information.

Opportunities for the research to through from web quests
What I know ha saying on the growth from the second key: "The volume from the information",a from the main potentialities from the technologies digital is the access to inform-ton diverse from the plus varied sources. From there what a axis central from the education on TIC be develop on the students the skills necessary for what perform searches

Pertinent, reflexive and critical according to the needs or pedagogical objectives, so-social or cultural issues that arise.

Web quests and scavenger hunts are useful tools to guide students. Students in the processes of searching, selecting and analyzing information and in the use of it, for the resolution of problems or work slogans.

The pedagogical integration of these resources requires teachers to cut clear of the topic to treat; formulate questions and goals according to the scope of the project, the student possibilities and available sources; do an exploratory job tin and selection of relevant information sources and structure the tool in a series of steps that will organize the tasks to be carried out by the different work teams. Under. For the presentation of these activities, word processors may be used, software specific or templates *online*. The sources from information to Consult they canbe hosted on the intranet installed at the school, on different CDs, digital encyclopedias,such and/or websites. It can also be considered non-digitized information, written, audiovisual, and sound and speech.

The search and selection from information and the reflection guided to through from are tool-These are valuable initial experiences that will allow students to gradually reach progressively greater degrees of autonomy and self-regulation in their processes of interaction with information.

Web quest: synthesis from the tool

"Web quest" means inquiry and research through the Web and consists of a proposal that favors learning by guided discovery and the approach of atheme from a problematizing perspective. It is a tool that allows the teacher to give very specific and precise guidelines for students to carry out a search through different sources of information.

Frequently, a question is asked that alludes to a situation or scenario that requires to be analyzed from different positions, interests or perspectives to be understood as a complex phenomenon. In this sense, it gives the possibility of being able to be used in cross-cutting projects. The tool offers opportunities for students recognize, simulate and experience characters, conflicts, roles, tensions, changes or existing contradictions in the situations raised.

The web quest proposes a dynamic that aims at collaborative work. The groups perform chores differentiated but what converge on the achievement from a goal common. The in-dagations they can promote from slogans what point to the compilation or analysisfrom information, resolution from riddles, issue from lawsuits, building from consensusor production. The students are divided into groups, access the different sources that the teacher has proposed and select the information relevant on base to the chores what I knowthey have been presented.

The search from information on Internet, intranet, CD or others sources is a componentcentral of the web quest as a teaching proposal. However, its potential logic lies in the possibility of conveying processes that transform informationin knowledge. That is, in motorizing a set of actions such as identifyinginformation relevant to the objectives what I know must comply and organize it; discriminate

type of data; recognize information producing agencies; evaluate positioning cough or interests of the material presented by the sources; make conclusions about thetrouble what I know aims to understand and build up collectively a product end whatDemonstrate a possible solution and take students' positions.

The particularity that this tool has for the teacher is that it allows him, throughof a simple and attractive project, generate your own digital teaching materials adapted to his group from students and his context particular. Is important have on billthat the flow of information that circulates demands a certain updating of the sourcesidentified parties, the checking of their contents and the renewal of the slogans that they carry To the classroom.

Contributions pedagogical the job with web quests
Favors the job with supports multimedia.

Auspicious the access to sources from information varied and diverse.

Develop skills from research, search, selection, evaluation and hierarchy-tin of information around goals previously established.

Shape skills for the reading hyper textual and the understanding from texts.

Promotes the appropriate and ethical use of information regarding the fulfillment of objectives ties, the satisfaction of needs and the resolution of problems raised from prospects complex and decision making.

Incentivize the growth from skills from learning autonomous and collaborative.

It favors critical and creative thinking about information and the ability to "hyper reading".

Encourages the growth from skills metacognitive and from evaluation from processes.

Developing from the tool
As we expressed in previous paragraphs, the web quest is a tool designed bythe teacher, who integrates ICT and collaborative learning through inquiry guided by various sources of information, often hosted on the Web. It pre-It is presented in a digital format and is structured in clearly established parts to which what is

entered from from a navigation tree:

Introduction

Homework

Process

Evaluation

Conclusion

When a teacher develops a web quest and shares it with other colleagues, they can enterinclude a pulled apart, "Page the Professor". There I know explain the justification the cutoutof that field of knowledge and the global guidelines of the work that is attempted to be carried out with the students.

Introduction
Be which be the contents what I know want to work, is important what the web quest I know present-in an attractive way for the students. For this purpose, it is appropriate to ask a questioninitial what serve from "hook" for wake the interest from the students from the beginning.The introduction -clear and brief- should pose a situation problematic to sort out whatappeal to curiosity and imply a challenge.

Homework
It is one of the most important parts. The teacher will develop their ingenuity and creativity to think of interesting tasks that respond to the curricular objectives, avoiding the overabundance of instructions and guidelines.

Is important to focus on the understanding from one or two topical substantial what formpart the theme principal from the web quest. The proposal is design a homework authentic whatI carried to the transformation from the information avoiding the trend to the mere reproduction.

There are many categories of tasks to design a good web quest. Some examples-

Examples can be: solve a problem or mystery; formulate and defend a position; design a product; analyze a complex reality; produce a persuasive messagea journalistic treatment; collect information, etc.

Process
Is the part fundamental from a web quest well designed? The process should agree withthe description from the homework. Is confirmed by Steps what the students must perform,with the links included in each step.

It is a time to organize the complexity of the research proposal. The drafting of the process also requires the incorporation of another central principle of the web quests: the division into roles or perspectives, characteristics of collaborative learningtie. Here a set of well-structured and precise subtasks are defined for each task. One of the roles that the students will adopt.

The design from web quests have two challenges: achieve on are activities and Steps a true- deco scaffolding cognitive for the students and promote the negotiation from meaningsCome in the students after a collective production.

Resources
This section lists the websites previously selected so that users can students can to concentrate on the theme to inquire and avoid the navigation to the drift.

In reality, the resources can be presented in a separate section or be included in the process stage, in a general or personalized way, depending on the roles to be investigate. Many times, in addition to websites, it will be convenient to expand with other sources and suggest other types of resources such as magazines, books, surveys, diagrams etc.

Evaluation
The objective here is to promote group evaluation of the product and self-evaluation of individual achievements. An evaluation is required to be clear and concrete; This is more than a process of reflection, since it accompanies and guides learning by providing in information to know how to continuously

redirect the construction of the knowledge.

Requirements from management by part the teacher
Identify stages the draft curriculum, from classroom or institutional, on the I know will integrate the tool, taking into account its particularities and potentialities.

Design the activities with the tool having on bill a diversity from with-signs, interests, skills and access to multimedia resources.

Propose slogans what integrate different idioms (oral, written, audiovisual, hyper-textual) and speech genres (narrations, interviews, reports, etc.).

Define topic, general objective, contents and key concepts in a simple way, which allow complex problems to be addressed from a multiplicity of perspectives (demystify stereotypes, the job with the multicausality, identify components

Subjective in the production of information and construction of knowledge, emphasizing in notions of dynamic processes, etc.)

Carry out a search exploratory from material available on the theme on sites Web, CD or others materials digital, and the check from their possible changes, updates andof the validity of the material. Contemplate the opportunities to generate collaborative dynamicsabortive with teachers of different subjects.

Assess the complexity of the content and structure of the identified sites (fa-ease navigation) and make a preselection of them.

Check the validity from the sources selected what resources to use.

Present the strategy to the students, divide them into groups, and specify the work group and the individual, and the moments from recapitulation on group big. Monitor theprocess and evaluate learning in each stage.

Carry out recaps systematic from topics, approaches, conclusions transitory, and from chores on groups, subgroups and with the group total to end from place them on the process global,in the production generated and in which they are required to perform.

Generate spaces for reflection and awareness of students regarding the co-knowledge, uses, meanings and opportunity of the tool in the project (inquire on practices frequent with TIC on scopes no schoolchildren; to debate on similarities anddifferences between the tool to work with and other known ones; reflect on the complementarity and the new applications from tools already acquaintances; anticipate facilitators,obstacles, controversies and risks what can arise at job with the tool).

Propitiate terms for generate searches from information relevant and S.I.G-nificative (motivate the genuine interest of the students; define objectives that integrate curricular guidelines with student concerns; select priority sources reinforcing scientific rigor, reliability of information, style of language, esthetic, the wealth from material multimedia, etc.; favor the use flexible but effective the time, promote the emergence of new concerns or questions from the search is scheduled and that can be taken up in subsequent activities; encourage instances playful and creative what open to the emotions, the expressiveness and the imagination on turnstileto the topic being addressed.

Plan modes from communication, archive and communication from the productions really-given by the students.

Recommendations alternatives for the case from no exist Connection to the Net
The web quest is, what already I know ha saying, a tool digital what organize the searchinformation on different websites. However, the navigable conditions I know they can generate on an intranet. In addition, the pages what I know go to use and linkthey can Get down and copy on a processor from text for later perform the hyperlinks corresponding and maintain them even when there is no Internet, always maintain keeping the reference to the source in question. Search slogans, too,they can refer to digital encyclopedias or to other CD-ROMs.
Difference with others tools for the research
The treasure hunt, also called a "treasure hunt", is another tool of search guided from information. Consists on a sheet from route what presents a Series from questions about a topic and a list of places (files or websites) where students they can find us the answers. Frequently, as closure of the development of the activity

and as a conclusion, an integrating question is included that facilitates the organization of the collected information. Unlike the web quest, the process of search that is proposed has a more linear sequence and does not aim to put into play the diversity of prospects.

The road map of a treasure hunt can be made with a processor of text, presentation software or *online templates.* The places to search they can be housed on the internet installed on the school, on different CD me on sitesinternet website.

This is a useful strategy to present content, to deepen knowledgearound a topic and to assess learning. Can be considered as an activity group, individually or combining both modalities.

Opportunities
For the communication to through from weblog
Some of the pedagogical potentialities of ICT are to improve the skillsdes from communication from the students, generate new shapes from expression and propitiatethe participation on the lifetime public. Through the technologies digital I know originate new perspectives of interrelation with others, which can strengthen the construction of identities individual and collective, and favor the production Social the knowledge.

As we stated in previous sections, for an adequate training of the new generations is indispensable what the school no alone teach to investigate and organize cri-ethically and creatively the information, but also that it gives the opportunities to produceinformation and culture.

For the development of the communicative function from the use of ICT in the field school I know ha selected, to mode from example, a Format specific from immense I grew up-ment today: the weblog, also called "blog" or "log".

Weblog: synthesis from the tool
Exist diverse to form from conceive the weblog. These they may be thought what:

A publication on line characterized by the configuration chronological reverse from thetickets, on the what I know pick up, to mode from daily, links, news and opinions from authorshipmainly single with a casual style and subjective. [48]

A space for asynchronous communication, generally designed to express ideas or opinions from a written format, although you can also display photos, graphs, cos and drawings, audio or video sequences. [49]

A communication system where everyone is editors, collaborators and critics, for- I command a multidirectional scheme of exchanges. A weblog is a web page dynamic in which visitors actively participate. Fifty

Blogs allow you to combine various forms of communication, languages and also re-courses from Internet. Serving What seeker because allow pose links specific with others sites linked to the theme what I know tries [51] , I know they look like to the e-mail by the style informal from communicationwhat I know uses with frequency on they and I know resemble to the forums from opinion already what the readers can-give take part on the building the theme or debate contributing their comments [52] .The possibility of having, without special technical knowledge, a form ofplication on line, the gratuity, the ease from access, the possibility from insert linksor links and his interactivity [53] They are some from the features and functions what facilitatehis adoption in the educational field.

On terms general, the weblog must be considered tools by means, medium from the students they build knowledge on interaction with the others. I know treats from a opportunitydad for what the students play a paper active what allow give bill from the processes what experience, reply to concerns own and from the rest, to emit opinions, generate discussion, contribute some information and to intervene on their contexts from lifetime. Chance formanifest their interests, needs, certainties, Doubts and interpretations on some theme in particular. From the creation of weblogs, the students become, then, in authors, producers from contents and providers from information. Perform observations,questions and answers. Dan and get *feedback,* I know connect, they help to filter information.Have the possibility from take the weather for to think, organize the ideas [54.]

Contributions pedagogical from work with weblog
Favors the job with supports multimedia.

Develop the skills communicative and new shapes expressive from the studentsto through new formats.

Shape skills for the writing hyper textual and the production from materials multimedia.

Favors the management from the overabundance from information for extract sense from is.

Develop the reading review, the skills from search and evaluation from information,and the adoption of selection criteria for reliable sources.

Gets better the skills of understanding and of Text production.

It encourages autonomous and collaborative learning, favoring the development of skillscities metacognitive and the evaluation of processes.

Promotes the proper use and ethical from information, as well as the taking of decisions.

Facilitates the exchange with the others (companions, teachers, members from the communitynearby or remote cities).

Strengthens the building from the identities individual and collective.

Develop the creativity.

Strengthens a pedagogy Focused on student.

Developing from the tool
The weblog they are tools from communication, multimedia, interactive, flexible anddynamic. Allow to integrate idioms, contents and resources on turnstile to a diversityof purposes. According to the nature of the material that is published, they are classifiedin photo blogs, video blogs, audio blogs and mob logs (content that has been captured from mobile or cellular telephony). They are characterized by their frequent updates andbecause favor the communication from character

multidirectional The blogging They are spacesfor the expression of the authors, in which readers can actively participate doing comments, thus becoming your co-creators.

Some from the activities necessary for the production from a blog they are the search,the reading, the selection and the interpretation from information on a theme. Is by itthat the use of this tool in pedagogical proposals is a primary way privileged registration, systematization and documentation of construction processesindividual and social the knowledge. The interaction with is shape from publication and fromvirtual social exchange allows students to start a process in which they gradually mind I know go making experts on a matter and by the what they can reach to becomeon source of information and reference for other blogs that address the same topic .

Edit and to post a blog it implies place on play a Series from skills referredto the organization of information, expression and reflection on the processes of communication [56]. First, blogs allow you to organize information by creating categories and chains from information to through from links Come in they. These procedure-cough favor the retrieval and application of information on the topics to be discussed, problems to sort out. From East mode, the weblog I know convert on a chance for

Manage the overabundance from information on internet [57], contextualize and organize thespeech on shape hyper textual. What's more, is possible say what are structures from public-cation on the Internet, and the elements that make them up, give rise to innovative ways narratives and generate new practices for to debate and to argue.

In the same way, blogs can be conceived as a valuable space for expression; exchange and participation social, politics and cultural from the students. The choice thetitle of the blog, the topic, the perspective from which the content is approached, the choice from sources, the information personal/collective what I know offers, the directories on the what I knowregister, the design used, the colors, sounds or images selected, the linksof the blogroll or the comments are the resources that a weblog provides to strengthen, express and communicate identity. A weblog takes public status on the Net by opening space for the circulation of ideas regarding who and how their authors or readers are.On what vision of world they own, what motivates them or what worries them

A) Yes, East Format contributes to the gets better from the skills communicative and from expression. The authors generate articles with the aim of making known what they know, think and feel, and readers actively participate by leaving their comments. This dynamic means that texts have to be produced clearly enough to be included by the the rest (be these teachers, students or the community on general). Dialogue with others, for its part, provides useful information for self-regulation.tion and monitoring of the learning process itself. Unlike other tools that support conversations, such as forums, weblogs give authors a peace personal and, simultaneously, a space Social. Is say, "grant a space for the reflection individual, for the record from the evolution from the ideas to it length the weather, for multiple connections and exchange in different spaces" [58]. Similarly, the communicability of a message becomes an object of reflection for those studentswho want to be heard.

In addition, the utilization the blog enables create and develop a new stage from expression that is necessary and valuable in two senses. First, because it is known that due to personal characteristics, fear of being wrong or difficulties in presenting in public [59], not all students participate in class and interactions are reduced to a small group. Creating and commenting on blogs allows you to speak on this sense. Second, organizing a weblog involves organizing ideas, setting a schedule, purpose, imagine and build a reader, express oneself, systematize a thought, etc. FromIn this way, the great benefit granted by this kind of "virtual genre" is that it brings the shape from "have voice on the Net" from way very simple. "Have voice", on sense A.M-ply, as a possibility of expression regarding the topics of interest of a person or a group and the extended communication of the same to other people with whom they do notshare a space, not a time.

Other skills that are developed during interaction with this type of up- plications virtual they are the from form on the new media from communication, create A reflection own, be a thinker critical, generate points from view alternative and contribute- take them to the others. Within the opportunities for reflection generated by working with weblog I know opens a strong line from training and debate on turnstile to the "ethics" from thosethat produce. Legal frameworks, freedom of expression, respect for different ideas, you see, the analysis from the situations social, the reflection about from the shapes adequatefrom expression on turnstile to the objectives and contexts on the what they will circulate the posts They aretopical centers of training on this tool [60] .

Exists a diversity from weblog intended to ends educational or *edibles*. Some fromthem are created by:

Teachers [61,] to establish a space for asynchronous communication with the students. Through this medium, teachers can schedule li- guidelines for the realization from chores, to open a space virtual from questions andcomments, Send activities, bibliography and links to sites Web from consultation.

Teacher *weblogs* are the ones used for communication, in- sharing, planning, research and collective production among peers (educational materials; multidisciplinary projects, systematization con- teaching practice board, etc.).

Students, to publicize individual school experiences and collective. These blogs can comment on activities carried out, present documents from job, organize collaboratively a research, an-rar the development of projects and their results. These are spaces that allow feedback from the teacher exclusively and/or from their peers. In relation to individual work, an ex- experience that can be very interesting is the personal log of the student. This registration can be prolonged during the entire transit through the school, empowering the building from the identity and the tracing from theown story.

Teachers and students in the classroom, to work by disciplines or in projects multidisciplinary or transverse. The blogging from classroom favor so muchgroup work within a course, such as between courses and schools. They can use be stored in a variety of ways, such as a class diary, notebook, or digital *portfolio.*

Members from the *institution school,* for give bill from his history, ideology, Projects, links with the community, etc.

It is necessary to take into account that given the potential of blogs to be a space for the visibility public, the production from the students is on terms from transcend-right the classroom. A Blog can be a chance from interaction with others spaces insidefrom school, other schools, organizations or communities nearby or distant.

Structure the blog

A blog is formed by various components [62]:

Header: is the Name or qualification what the or the authors assign to the blog. Can-to contain an image.

Categories or themes: system that allows you to organize the contents of the blog according to the criteria established by its author. In general, these categories are they are located in a column to the side of the central body of the blog.

Article, post or entry: it constitutes the central body of writing of a bi- Tacoma. Depending on the publication system that has been selected for to work, the tickets or *posts* I know identify with date from publication and category to the one they belong to.

Comments: the option from comment the tickets It allows to the visitor let their opinion on the content exposed in these, clarify what is read or expand it with new data, links or reflections. Each blog entry is in itself a small forum. Comments allow visitors to provide feedback, complementmen and improve articles.

Trackbacks - This component, also called a cross- *reference, dada* or *inverse, backlink* or *inverse link,* is an element that is part of the content of some of the blog publishing systems and serves to let him know to the Author from a Blog what on other Blog I know ha included a *link* or link what it binds with any from their articles. TO times I know it uses when I know wants make a comment on a content and it is preferred to do it on the blog itself to can spread more.

Syndication from contents (RSS) or aggregators from news: Thank you to they, a user can read the news of all the blogs he wants without having to visittar them one to one; So, by example, a Professor can read everything it what their students have posted on their blogs just by adding them to your list.

Requirements from management by part the teacher

Define the target general, set up the theme and type from draft what will have the blogor blog for the development of the pedagogical proposal.

Conduct exploratory searches of blogs, websites, CDs, or other direct materials. Vitals that deal with the subject and/or pose the same objectives. Select materials according to their level of complexity and relevance, which serve as inputs for the growth of a weblog for educational purposes.

To select the type from binnacle what will develop with their students (individual, groupor collective; open or closed).

Design the dynamic from interaction Come in the weblog and his integration to the job on the classroom.
generate spaces for the reflection and sensitization from the students respect the know-I lie, applications and senses on turnstile to the tool on the draft (inquire on practices frequent with ICT in non-school settings; discuss similarities and differences between the tool to work and other known ones; reflect on the complementarity dad and the new applications from tools already acquaintances; anticipate facilitators, obstacles,controversies and risks that may arise at work with the tool).

Propitiate terms for the writing from the weblog (to motivate the interest genuine from thestudents; build climates of trust; define objectives that integrate curricular guidelineslaser with concerns from the students; favor a use flexible but effective the weather onthe classroom what contemplate the periods necessary for the creation; favor a first moment- to for the expression and newly a second weather for the correction grammatical or spelling; foment the autocorrect, the reading Come in pairs and the rewrite; favor instances from analysis from productions and the reflection on the plurality from interpretations; foment ins- trances playful and creative what open to the emotions and the imagination on turnstile to the theme that I know board; respect the shapes diverse from organize the information; to integrate codes andmodalities from expression own from the youths with the what I know works).

Use this innovative form of communication to monitor the learning process. Teaching, carry out interventions to improve learning, send guidelines and materials of work, and assess the learning of the students.

Encourage the creation from communities from learning:

Generate instances to share information and express personal ideas as a way to improve teaching and learning processes. Set up a new channel communication between teachers and students.

Promote spaces for to interact with their pairs teachers with the target from com-share experiences, exchange materials, plan together and carry out research.

Institutionally define the publication criteria.

Propose updating dynamics according to the possibilities of the project, of the students and resources.

Generate spaces for reflection on ethical issues and responsibility in the generationration of content and in the process of social communication.

Guide students in design processes and communicability.

Generate spaces of reflection on the credibility building.

Foresee moments for learn to handle the tool on growing degrees from com-laxity. Promote a flexible and efficient use of time. Take into account the deadlines production of work, both individual and group [63].

Differences with others tools for the communication

The most notable distinction between blogs and traditional web pages is that the former generate instances of greater interactivity with their readers (entry of comments) and relationship with other blogs and websites (inclusion of referencescrossovers or *trackbacks)*. The prevailing communicative model is bidirectional in blogs and unidirectional on web pages. In the latter case, the information from the author to the readers. There are some that have more dynamic spaces, such as including email, and others also include, as one more element, a blog. The weblogs are frequently updated, thanks to the ease of editing and to post. What's more, the archive from the information on order chronological reverse and the Indi-cation of new inputs simplify the access to the information and your reading.

With relationship to the difference with the forums from discussion I know highlights what "The possibility from interaction provided by weblogs is complementary to the function of forums. These are still very valid to stimulate debates within a work group. TheBlogs, however, are more useful in organizing the conversation if what is aims to is to contribute new data and links (Wise,

2005)" [64].

Finally, web quests differ from weblogs mainly in the format and the presentation structure of the proposal. The weblog organizes the publication by dates from every event, while what the web quests I know find organized with axis onthe bar from navigation what introduce to the student in the Actions to perform. Bibliography.

www.ingramcontent.com/pod-product-compliance
Lightning Source LLC
LaVergne TN
LVHW051715050326
832903LV00032B/4208

* 9 7 9 8 4 3 5 7 1 9 1 4 7 *